The Changing Face of Bishop's Waltham

by Alan Inder

Reproduced with permission from Hampshire County Council's Rights of Way section.

Map legend:
- ▬ Parish boundary
- ▬ Footpath
- ▬ Bridleway
- ▪▪▪ Restricted Byway

1:25,000

The Changing Face of Bishop's Waltham

First published 2011. Published by the Bishop's Waltham Society and the Bishop's Waltham Museum Trust.

ISBN: 978-0-9511449-1-6

Acknowledgements

This book has grown from the original concept to something far more ambitious, and I acknowledge gratefully the assistance of those without whom the ambition would not have been fulfilled.

In particular I would like to thank **John Grover**, not only for his amazing knowledge of the town centre and its many characters but also his steady guidance throughout; **Nigel Auckland** has used his photographic skills to take many of the 2011 photographs and do much of the scanning that had to be done; **Tony Kippenberger** has provided very useful editorial abilities and experience; and **Neil Gibbons** has used his considerable graphic design expertise to help with the layout, design and publication of the document. Behind the scenes, in the Museum, volunteers have helped with locating images and researching information. And in some parts of the book we have depended on 'Bishops Waltham: Parish, Church and Town', so well researched by **Peter Watkins**.

Many thanks to you all. Without your help we would not be having the pleasure of looking through this book now.

Alan Inder
September 2011

Inside front cover: *The southern part of the High Street, looking towards St George's Square from Cross Street, c1900.*

Page 1: *Bank Street in 1912, on the left, blending into the High Street, 2011.*

This page: *Map of Bishop's Waltham Parish.*

Page 3: *Aerial view of Bishop's Waltham from the east, taken c2006.*

Contents

Introduction

Bishop's Waltham is a small medieval town in Hampshire, situated roughly midway between Winchester and Fareham. Like many small towns in southern England, Bishop's Waltham has undergone many changes over the past 150 years, particularly in the past four decades.

This book sets out to record and illustrate the main changes that have occurred. Several books, notably those by Barbara Biddell and Peter Watkins, have shown admirably how the town has changed in social and economic terms. This book aims to complement those previous books by focusing primarily on changes to the physical environment, i.e. the structure and layout of the settlement, the alterations to the townscape and setting of the town, the new roads and buildings, etc.

It is a story about major changes to Bishop's Waltham, balanced to some extent by scenes that have barely altered in the past 100 years. In spite of the changes that have occurred - and not all have been for the better - Bishop's Waltham is still an attractive place to live and to visit. Most of all it has a remarkable vitality and an extraordinary community spirit. Long may it last. Let us hope that community spirit and pride in this lovely small town survives the further changes that will inevitably come.

In 1986 the eminent local historian John Bosworth produced a book entitled *Bishop's Waltham & Newtown: 25 Years of Change*. My original idea for this book was to update John's book using a similar format and looking at further changes in the 25 years up to 2011. However, this concept was abandoned early on, partly because so few of the photographs in the 1986 book still exist in reproducible quality but mainly because searches of the Bishop's Waltham Museum's archives revealed some very good photographs going back 120 years or more, some of them featuring scenes not covered in the 1986 book. By using the additional resources found in the Museum's collection I hope to show even more clearly how Bishop's Waltham has evolved. It is a fascinating story and I hope it will give enlightenment and enjoyment to all readers of the book.

This book has been produced as a result of collaboration between the Bishop's Waltham Society, Bishop's Waltham Museum Trust, myself and other individuals. We would like to dedicate it to the memory of two people who gave so much to researching and recording the recent history of Bishop's Waltham, and making it accessible to, and enjoyable by, residents and visitors alike:

John Bosworth (1937 - 2005)

John was a quiet, humble man who lived in Bishop's Waltham all his life and dedicated much of his adult life to photographing the changes that were going on, as well as many events and people. He also collected postcards and photographs taken by others, and it has been said that his collection of pictures of the town amounted to more than 20,000 images. Although only a small fraction of that collection still exists in the local Museum, it forms the basis of this book, and we owe him our gratitude for that.

Bill Walmsley (1929 - 2011)

Bill came to Bishop's Waltham late in life, but he devoted much of his retirement to improving the town and helping to interpret its history to others. One of his many good projects was to get the Millennium Clock installed in The Square. Bill died while this book was being prepared, but as we turn its pages there are scenes that will bring back memories of his hard work, undertaken for the sake of the community into which he so happily settled.

We have tried to ensure that the information in the book is as accurate and complete as possible. If you have any missing information or would like to correct any errors, please contact the Bishop's Waltham Museum via its website **www.bishopswaltham.net/museum** so that any revised edition can be improved.

Alan Inder *(September 2011)*

Top: *The Millennium Clock in The Square, an iconic feature of Bishop's Waltham that owes much to Bill Walmsley's vision and dedication.*

Centre right: *Very few close up photos of John Bosworth exist!*

Bottom right: *Bill and Irene Walmsley in later years.*

Bottom left: *John Bosworth, captured in typical mode, walking round Bishop's Waltham (in Bank Street) with a camera around his neck!*

Page 4: *Aerial view of Bishop's Waltham from the east, taken in April 1951. Beyond the town centre is the medieval Bishop's Waltham Pond. At the top right of the picture is the brick and tile works and claypit at Claylands. (Copyright: English Heritage).*

A Brief History

Bishop's Waltham is a small market town situated 11 miles south-east of Winchester, at the junction between the chalk downs to the north and the London Clay of south Hampshire's coastal plain. The original settlement was built on gently rising ground between the two main sources of the River Hamble at Northbrook and The Moors.

The town gets its name from the Bishop's Palace that was built in the 12th century and "Waltham", the "settlement in the forest" (Saxon).

The town was laid out by the Bishop of Winchester, Henry de Blois, in the area to the north-east of the Palace, at the same time as the palace was rebuilt (c1160-70). The grid comprises four streets that are aligned north-east to south-west (Brook Street, High Street, Houchin Street, and Basingwell Street) that are linked by small cross lanes. Along the top and bottom of the grid are Bank Street and The Square, respectively. St Peter's Church also dates from the 12th century and was sited on higher ground to the north east of the town centre. Thus it was located on the fringe of the settlement, and did not form an integral part of the plan. St Peter's Street, which was developed by the 14th century, links the grid of streets to the parish church to the north.

For centuries, Bishop's Waltham was dominated by, and also benefitted from, the Bishop's Palace which was one of the great palaces of medieval England. As a result, the rather compact centre and its Church formed the basis of a large, and relatively important, medieval village. For instance, Bank Street was originally known as French Street probably because French merchants lived and ran their businesses there. Servicing the Palace would have been a strong commercial draw not commonly found in country villages during the Middle Ages.

After the destruction of the Palace in the middle of the 17th century, and the consequent loss of status, Bishop's Waltham became a commercial and service centre for the agricultural community of the district. As a medieval village it remained virtually unchanged from the 12th century to the second half of the 19th century. Then two significant developments happened, simultaneously, that helped turn it into the small market town it is today.

Left: *Tithe Map, 1841*

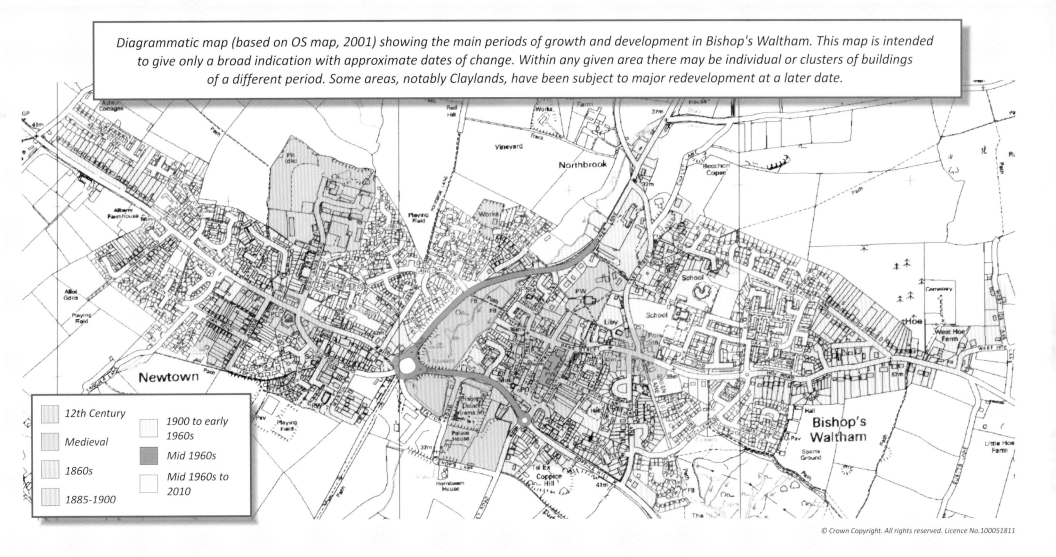

Diagrammatic map (based on OS map, 2001) showing the main periods of growth and development in Bishop's Waltham. This map is intended to give only a broad indication with approximate dates of change. Within any given area there may be individual or clusters of buildings of a different period. Some areas, notably Claylands, have been subject to major redevelopment at a later date.

Legend:
- 12th Century
- Medieval
- 1860s
- 1885-1900
- 1900 to early 1960s
- Mid 1960s
- Mid 1960s to 2010

Claylands Brick and Tile Works

In the 1860s Arthur Helps, who had political and royal connections, established the Bishop's Waltham Clay Company and began extracting clay from fields on the Vernon Hill estate to the west of the town. At the end of what is now Claylands Road, industrial buildings were built for the production of bricks and tiles, terracotta, and fine art pottery. Because of the influx of workers, the suburb of Newtown was developed, with rows of houses, a school, pubs, and so on. After Mark Henry Blanchard took over the works in 1871 a period of expansion followed, and in its heyday Claylands became the most important brick and tile works in Hampshire.

The Bishop's Waltham Railway

In 1863 a branch line was built from Botley, on the Eastleigh to Fareham railway line, to Bishop's Waltham. Arthur Helps, who was responsible for getting the brick and tile works under way, was also instrumental in bringing the railway to Bishop's Waltham. Sidings were laid from the Station to the Claylands works, for the transport of raw materials and finished products, and to the Gas Works (for which Helps was also responsible) at the end of Garfield Road. The coming of the railway underpinned a period of prosperity for Bishop's Waltham.

For the first half of the 20th century, there were no further major developments in Bishop's Waltham. However, all that was to change, markedly.

Post War expansion: Roads and Parking

In the 1950s Bishop's Waltham went into decline, as reported in an article in 1953 in the weekly *Illustrated Magazine* entitled 'Town that is Dying'. During that decade Gunners Bank, the Brewery in Lower Lane, the Mill on the road to Waltham Chase, and the two brickworks at Claylands and Coppice Hill all closed, and the ambulance service and fire brigade were withdrawn. The County Court was no longer held in the town. By the mid 1960s there were many shops for sale, the railway line had closed, buses and cars choked the High Street, and there was no off-street parking. There was still no main sewerage.

The town needed radical change, but perhaps few people were prepared for the drastic changes that followed. In the period from 1965 to 1970 the town changed more than at any time since the 12th century.

Firstly, through traffic was largely removed from the town centre by constructing an inner bypass, in two sections:

1) From the junction of the Botley and Wickham roads westwards to Winchester Road, by driving a new road through the old courtyard at the rear of the Crown, and the outer courtyard and stables of the Palace, and across the Great Pond, severing it in two, to a large new roundabout (on the site of the old Station) at the junction of Winchester and Victoria Roads;

2) From the new roundabout northwards towards Corhampton and Alresford, along the trackbed of the old railway line to a new junction with Lower Lane.

Secondly, the problem of lack of off-street parking was solved by forming the central car park to the east of the High Street. This involved much demolition of buildings on the east side of Houchin Street, the west side of Basingwell Street, and the whole of Red Lion Street. In the process many buildings of local architectural and historic interest were demolished, and the evicted residents were moved to the new Ridgemede housing estate on the road to Swanmore, contributing to the loss of the close-knit community in the town.

Roads such as Houchin Street and Basingwell Street were widened and, in the words of Trevor Harvey (first Chairman of the Bishop's Waltham Society), Bishop's Waltham lost its "quality of cosy enclosure".

New Housing

Bishop's Waltham has expanded substantially in the past 50 years. The town grew in population from less than 3000 in 1961 to around 6700 in 2007. The initial spur for this growth was the provision of mains sewerage following the opening of Brooklands Farm Sewage Treatment Works in 1962.

The accretion of housing estates around the fringe of the historic town centre has been fairly modest (for instance Middlebrook, Malvern Close, Eastways, Southfields Close). Further afield some large estates have been built, for example the local authority estates at Battery Hill and Ridgemede, and the estates of private housing at Pondside (from 1973), Hermitage Heights, the area south of Winchester Road (for instance Siskin Close, and Elizabeth Way), off Free Street (for example Colville Drive and Hall Close), and off Hoe Road (for instance estates such as Hamble Springs and Cherry Gardens, off Cricklemede).

Other Changes

During this period the town lost through demolition a number of houses and other buildings of character, though not necessarily architecturally distinguished, including The Priory, Claylands House, Eastway House, Church House (Holm Oak), and the United Reformed Church in Lower Lane. These were some of the casualties of a time of growth that was not painless.

There has also been steady erosion of the relatively unspoilt rural character of Bishop's Waltham through road widening, the provision of pavements and street lights, and other such measures that have slowly but surely had an urbanising effect.

Another insidious change that has harmed the character of Bishop's Waltham, as in most towns and villages in England, has been the growth in car ownership and use; this is evident not only through the noise and fumes but also visually through on-street parking. It was difficult to photograph street scenes for this book in 2011, to compare with those of the past, without parked cars intruding. However, their presence helps to show the reality of modern life.

Comparison of many of the 'then' and 'now' photographs shows another change in the town's character that is, perhaps, surprising: there are far more trees than there were. This may be because of deliberate planting in some locations but in other places it is more likely that natural vegetation has thrived through lack of land management.

Above: Terraced houses in Beaufort Drive on the Pondside estate, built in the mid-1970s.

Facing page top: The 'central car park' between Basingwell and Houchin Streets provides good access to the High Street.

Facing page centre: The inner bypass, built across the Bishop's Waltham Pond in the late 1960s, helped to remove traffic from the town centre. The large roundabout in the distance was built on the site of the Railway Station.

Facing page bottom: A smart terrace of houses in Battery Hill, originally built as Council houses c1960. Many are now privately owned.

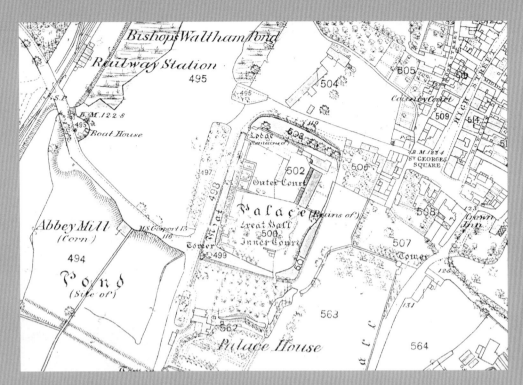

The Palace

In late Saxon times Winchester was the ecclesiastical centre of the kingdom of Wessex. Subsequently the bishops of Winchester ranked among the most senior bishops in England during the medieval period and beyond.

They were possessors of vast landed wealth on a princely scale - their estates reached through seven counties in the south of England from Surrey to Somerset, and from the Isle of Wight to Oxfordshire, and included over 60 manors, only half of which were in Hampshire. The income from these estates made the diocese the wealthiest in England in the medieval period and it is said that 'in the whole Christian world only the diocese of Milan was worth more'.

The Bishops were also powerful, as they were statesmen holding important offices under the crown. Henry de Blois (1090-1171) was the first of these bishop-statesmen and he was well connected, being related to William the Conqueror and King Stephen. He was appointed Bishop of Winchester in 1129, and had huge local estates that included Wolvesey (Winchester), Alresford, East Meon and Marwell, and, of course, Bishop's Waltham, where he began building the Palace in 1136, on a rectangular site surrounded by a bank and ditch.

Left: The First Edition OS map (1870) shows the layout of Palace ruins in the setting of the walled enclosure, and in relation to the town centre to the north east.

Right: The main range of buildings from near the Palace Farmhouse; from left to right: the West Tower, Great Hall, service rooms and kitchen.

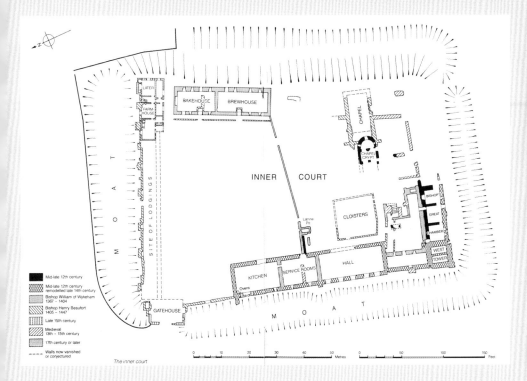

The inner court

Most medieval Bishops of Winchester contributed to the alteration and enlargement of this Palace, especially William of Wykeham who, between 1379 and 1401, rebuilt the Great Hall and provided a new Great Chamber, brewhouse and bakehouse, kitchen, and gatehouse. The next Bishop of Winchester, Henry Beaufort, heightened the West Tower (1404), built a new Chapel and a lodging range including the Dower House (1438-43). Thomas Langton (Bishop of Winchester from 1493 to 1501) built a brick wall around the site, enclosing The Lord's Garden, and corner turrets on the south and east sites.

Bishop's Waltham Palace was one of the greatest palaces of medieval England, and was visited by kings and queens including Richard the Lionheart, Henry V and Queen Mary. However, after nearly 500 years, the Palace came to a sudden and dramatic end in 1644 during the Civil War. It was besieged by parliamentary troops, abandoned, and then destroyed. Subsequently, the Palace became a source for building materials, and several houses in Bishop's Waltham contain material originally obtained from the Palace.

Today the impressive ruins are a Scheduled Ancient Monument in the care of English Heritage, open to the public daily from May to the end of September.

Top left: *The more detailed layout plan (provided courtesy of English Heritage) shows the uses of the various buildings and the approximate periods of construction.*

Top right: *The eastern range of buildings, which once housed the bakehouse and brewhouse. The red brick building that is partly visible to the left is the Palace Farmhouse, in which the Bishop's Waltham Museum is now housed.*

Bottom right: *Patterns of brick, stone and flint on the south wall of the Palace Farmhouse.*

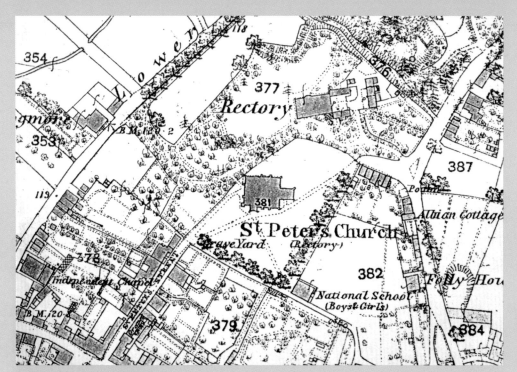

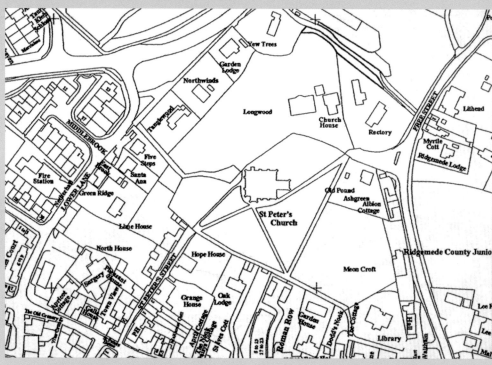

The Church

The first Saxon church was built in Waltham sometime between 680 and 725.

Typically a timber-framed building with wattle and daub walls and a thatched roof, there is no clear evidence for where it was situated. But it was from this church that St Willibald set out, probably around 720, to spread Christianity to heathen Germany. He later became Bishop of Eichstatt.

The original church was burned down as was the settlement in 1001 when Danes swept through the area. St Peter's Church itself was founded in the middle of the 12th century by Bishop Henry de Blois. It was built on a locally prominent site, on rising ground to the north of the town, possibly on the site of the much earlier church.

Very little remains of the original 12th century building. The north arcade, dating from c1200, is the oldest surviving part of the building (although the piers were renewed in the 19th century). The chancel, by William of Wykeham, is late 14th century. The west end of the church was rebuilt in 1849, and the south aisle was "restored" in 1897.

Left: The old map shows the Rectory as a substantial house to the north of the Church, with its stables block to the east.

Right: In the early 1960s the Church authorities decided to sell the Rectory and build a new, smaller one in the grounds, next to Free Street. The former stables was converted in 1994 to provide a parish meeting room and an office for the Church. The old Rectory is now a private house called Longwood.

Above: St Peter's Church from the south, probably in the early 1890s.

Top right: From the same viewpoint today, the most obvious change to the church building is the absence of the dormer windows, removed during the "restoration" of 1896/7 by the eminent late Victorian architect Sir Thomas Jackson.

The church clock was originally made for the Bishop's Palace and was rescued and then installed in the church after the Palace was abandoned during the Civil War. It is reputed to have the second heaviest pendulum in the world and needs winding every three days.

Centre right: A postcard of the Church viewed from wooden entrance gates at the top of St Peter's Street c1905. The west wall with its large window, to the left of the tower, had been rebuilt in 1849. On the top of the tower is a round turret that dates from when the tower was rebuilt in the late 1500s.

Bottom right: The present metal gates were installed in 1911 in memory of the Reverend Archer-Shepherd, who had been curate at St Peter's. Trees have grown tall, and now partly obscure the view of the Church from the town centre approach. The war memorial just inside the gates commemorates those who died in the First and Second World Wars and the 1982 Falklands Campaign.

St Peter's Street

St Peter's Street is arguably the most architecturally pleasing street in Bishop's Waltham, with several attractive large houses, areas of cobblestones, and the absence of pavements, road signs and other paraphernalia of modern streets.

Top: The view down the street c1911 from just below the churchyard gates. The first house on the left is Hope House, once a select ladies' school that was forced to close because of the scandal caused when a young Napoleonic prisoner of war billeted in the town threw a love letter over the wall to one of the young ladies. Opposite is North House, originally a 17th century timber framed building, subsequently considerably altered and extended, but still a very attractive house.

Bottom: The view from the same position in 2011 shows that the street scene has changed little, apart from the parked cars, and retains the great charm that it had a century ago.

Facing page left: Taken in April 1962 looking up St Peter's Street from Bank Street. On the right is the side window to Askew's shop, surrounded by the enamel product signs that are so redolent of those days. Further up the street a couple stand next to an Austin A35 outside the Bunch of Grapes, a 17th century building with later alterations.

Facing page right: In the 2011 view the projecting window of the old shop still remains, although the shop closed long ago and has since been in residential use. The ambience of Askew's shop has been recreated in the Museum. The Bunch of Grapes is still a pub with great character and charm.

15

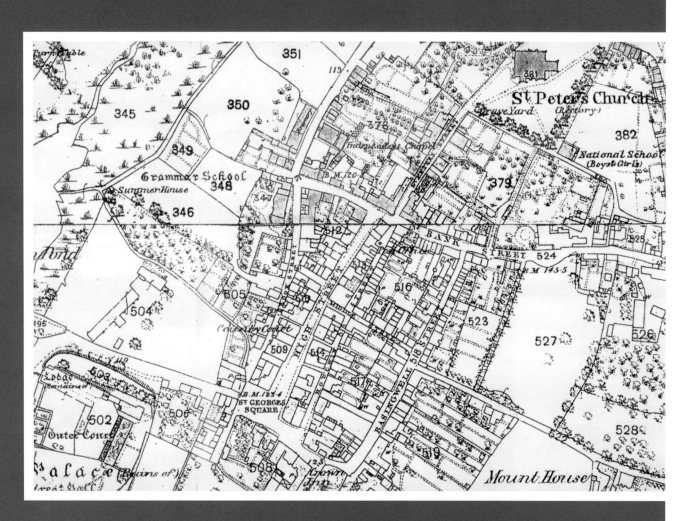

The Town Centre

The 1870 map shows just what a compact town centre Bishop's Waltham still had at that time. Clearly visible are the four original streets laid out by Henry de Blois (Brook Street, High Street, Houchin Street, and Basingwell Street) joined across the top by Bank Street. By the 15th century at least the High Street had become the principal street, and Brook, Houchin and Basingwell Streets had become little more than back lanes. The property blocks on both sides of the High Street have the appearance of encroachment onto a market area. Other property plots, certainly on the east side of Basingwell Street, consisted of long, narrow plots typical of more planned development.

Left: *What is striking is that, in 1870, open fields and copses come right up to the houses built along the principal streets, including a field with a range of stables and other buildings associated with the Palace that lay just the other side of what was then Station Road. It is now occupied by the Esso petrol station, Budgens and Malt Lane, and the open space by Fox's Garden Machinery.*

Along the length of what is the North Pond today are just a row of open fields, while to the east there are more fields immediately behind the Basingwell Street gardens. The road from Winchester wound around the south of the Great Pond, looped past the Palace and then curved to the right to enter St George's Square from the west where it met the High Street. Those continuing their journey to Portsmouth or Botley exited the Square past the Crown Inn.

Right: *The present day map tells a very different story. Infill has occurred all the way around the centre. From Budgens and its car park, through Southfield Close and on to St Bonnet Drive, the open land on the west has gone as has the field and wooded area in the east that now comprises Malvern Close, Shore Crescent and the Jubilee Hall (in the grounds of Mount House). The only open areas left are the spaces within St Peter's Church graveyard or around Palace Mews in the south-west.*

One of the two dramatic changes that are well evidenced by these maps was the building of the by-pass that brought traffic from Winchester straight across the pond, separating what is now called South Pond from the larger North Pond, and taking traffic away from St Georges Square and around the back of the Crown Inn. This involved the demolition of many buildings to the south and east of St George's Square including Coal Yard Lane which ran from the Square to what is now Palace Mews.

The other dramatic change, the demolition of the houses between Houchin Street and Basingwell Street to create the present town centre car park, is clearly shown by the maps but is also well illustrated in the aerial photographs on page 18 (overleaf).

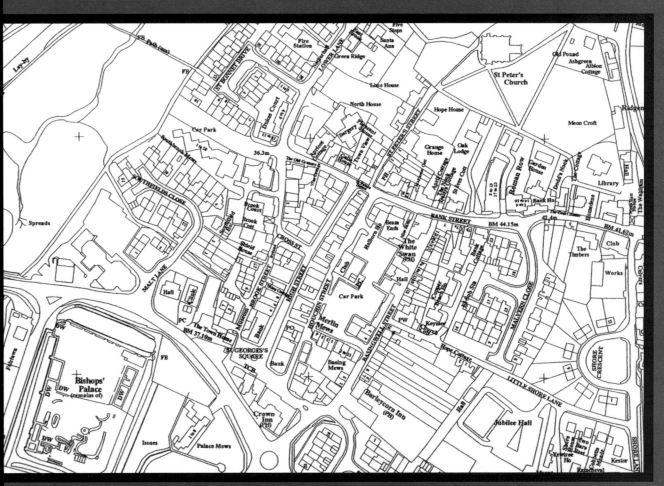

17

Top: *This aerial photograph was taken during or soon after the Second World War and beautifully captures Bishop's Waltham town centre at that time. The absence of traffic, only about half a dozen cars and a double-decker bus, and the fact that almost every garden appears to be growing rows of vegetables suggests that, at the very least, rationing is still in place.*

What is striking is the number of houses between Houchin Street and Basingwell Street that were demolished in the 1960s to create much needed car parking for the town. Although many of the dwellings in this area were considered not fit for human habitation by the 1960s (main sewerage did not arrive until 1962) a number of important old buildings were lost in the demolition process. (See pages 36 to 41 for more details).

Noticeable too are the clusters of building at the bottom and bottom left of the photo which disappeared with the construction of the bypass - practically none of the dozen or so buildings in that south-west corner remains. The same applies to the west of Brook Street where the houses and long gardens have given way to housing estates and other developments. Lower Lane has changed too, with the Brewery, the Congregational Chapel and the small public house on the corner being demolished in more recent years. Further along Lower Lane is the double-hipped roof of Middlebrook House, now the site of Middlebrook estate.

The tree-ringed field to the east, with a path across it and two browsing animals, is occupied by Malvern Close today. Down in the bottom right corner the Eastways estate has been built on the land which, at that time, was the site and gardens of Eastway House.

Bottom: *This present-day photograph, from a slightly different angle, shows the gap where houses were pulled down in the town centre to make way for the car park. On a happier note it also shows that a good number of the lime and copper beech trees around the field were saved when Malvern Close was built and have now reached considerable maturity. (Copyright Colin Waterworth, Capcha Photography).*

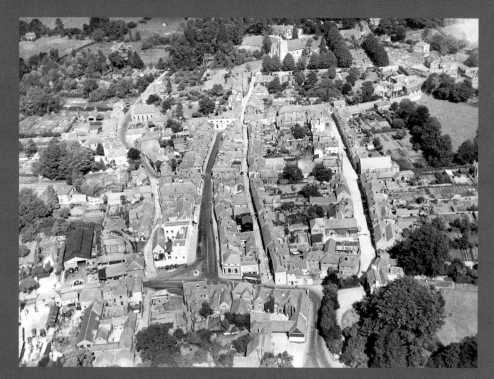

The High Street

Manorial records show that there has been a High Street since at least 1332 and many of the present day facades hide much older buildings.

Top: The top end of the High Street, c1910. A variety of small family-run shops front both sides of the street, and two imposing Georgian houses in Bank Street face down the shopping street.

Two boys and a dog stand in the road with little need to be concerned about road traffic. Beyond the lamppost on the right can be seen the sign for The Crow's Nest public house selling Alton Ales and Stout from what is now Lloyd's Pharmacy.

On the left is the original Padbury clock, placed there by James Padbury in 1864 to identify his shop and workshop in the premises below. James was the last of a family of renowned clockmakers who started their business in Bishop's Waltham in 1744; he died in 1898.

Bottom: Today there is still a good mix of shops and businesses, including many independent ones. In fact only three shops (Boots, Lloyds and the Co-op) in the northern part of the High Street belong to nationwide retail companies. Cars are more of a hazard as is the all too frequent parking on the double yellow lines.

The Padbury clock now only contains parts of the original after several renovations and accidents caused by high-sided lorries. But it is still wound up, one and a half times a week, from within a cupboard in the offices of SC Miller, accountants, who now occupy the first floor.

The hanging baskets are planted each year and looked after throughout the summer by Bishop's Waltham in Bloom.

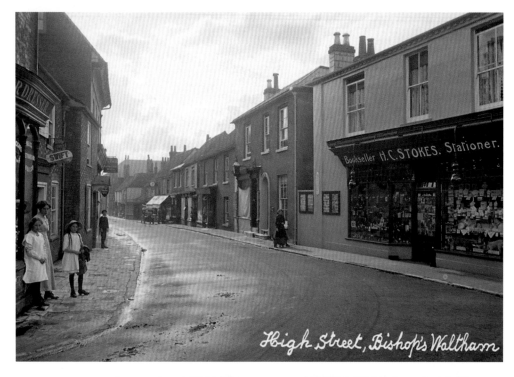

High Street, Bishop's Waltham

Left: *The view down High Street from Bank Street, probably around the time of the First World War. There was very little motorised traffic, and the road and pavements have yet to be improved. On the right, Mr Stokes had recently installed new windows; today the premises belong to Barrington's Delicatessen and the beautiful shopfront still exists. Further along the street, with the ornamental lamp outside, is a shop that had been a chemists since at least the 1830s. On the left, a young woman and two girls stand outside Mr Ware's hairdressers, and just beyond them is a tobacconists. The hairdressers is now a sweet shop, and the fine shopfront still exists.*

Below left: *Percy Dark, the dairyman at Butts Farm, with the milk float outside the dairy shop in the High Street about 1926. The shop had previously been the Crows Nest pub. Beyond the dairy shop is the shop of William Lang, tailor and outfitter.*

Below right: *Lloyds Pharmacy now occupy the premises, but apart from the modern fascia the frontage looks much the same. Lang's shop is now Tashinga.*

Facing page top left: *Mr Oliver's butcher's shop and Madeline's sweet shop in 1986, in a building that dates probably from the late 17th century; it had been the local Post Office in the early 1900s.*

Facing page bottom left: *By 2011 the building had been converted to a hairdresser's business, named after the sweet shop owner Madeline, who was a well known and popular High Street character. The building to the left was built in 1911 as the County Supply Stores, a grocery and hardware shop until it became Veck's furniture and carpet store in the 1960s; The Rowans Hospice charity shop took over from Veck's early in 2011.*

Facing page top right: *On the right of this view taken in 1959 is the Civic Cinema in the Oddfellows Hall, which was built in 1895 as a hall and meeting place for the Oddfellows Friendly Society (see Grand Opening, page 92) on the site of a grocer's shop. It became a cinema in about 1920, then in the mid-1970s it was acquired by Pullingers as a furniture showroom. Next to it was Mary's sweet shop, and in the red brick Georgian building beyond was the Country Stores.*

Facing page bottom right: *In the 2011 view, the former Oddfellows Hall has been The King's Church since 1995, the next building is occupied by Weller Patrick Estate Agents and the Coffee House. The former Country Stores has subsequently been owned by a series of wine merchants, making it possibly the oldest wine merchants' building in the country because wine has been sold on the premises continuously since 1617. By mid-2011 it had became Josie's Wine Shop and Deli.*

Top: *This scene shows some of the shops on the west side of High Street, and the entrance to Cross Street, c1917. From left to right are Giovanelli's sweet shop with the bicycle outside, Arthur Richards's gunsmith and jeweller next door, and The Bungalow Café on the far corner of the junction with Cross Street. The original black-faced Padbury clock (see page 19) visible just beyond the café has clearly been renovated because it now has a white face.*

Centre: *Mrs Veck (in pink) and Vi Hutchings stand outside what was then Stainer's bread shop in the early/mid 1960s. The former gunsmith and jeweller's shop had become a hardware shop, whilst across the road the Bungalow Café has changed hands and Belton & Hall are selling radios and TVs. Meanwhile, the clock above the jeweller's shop has disappeared as has the attractive bay window on its first floor, only to be replaced with disappointingly bland modern windows.*

Bottom: *In the comparable view in 2011, Andrew Grover stands outside the same premises, now a butcher's shop, after Stainer's moved to the Belton & Hall premises up the road, returning it to its use as a café and tea rooms. The shop to the right of Andrew is still a hardware shop (Morgan Hardware).*

Top and centre: *Views up the High Street from The Square, dated March 1963 and August 1967 respectively. The road signs in the left foreground show that through traffic still passed through the centre of Bishop's Waltham; the town centre bypass had not yet been built. The Civil Defence Centre, a real Cold War reminder, is clearly signposted in the earlier view.*

On the left is St George's House, which was a private residence until Barclays Bank took it over in 1921. On the right, SCATS (the Southern Counties Agricultural Trading Society) occupied what was originally a half-timbered building, mostly of 18th century construction, as was the Post Office building beyond.

In the 1967 photograph a bus shelter and sign can just be made out in front of Barclays main door. In the earlier photograph, the painted road markings, so visible in the aerial photograph on page 18, can still just be discerned around where the learner driver has parked his pick-up truck. Clearly they had been painted out once a shelter marked the stop.

Further along the street the 1967 photograph just shows that Southsea Building Supplies Ltd occupied what is, today, Hylands fruit and vegetable shop. The scene also shows that Mary's sweet shop on the left (with a Walls ice cream sign outside) was in direct competition with Madeline's sweet shop on the right-hand side of the High Street (with its sign for Bristol cigarettes).

Bottom: *The view from the same location in 2011 has changed little over the past 50 years or more, apart from the removal of the traffic island and the increase in parked cars. The Bank and Post Office remain in the same buildings, but the Co-op has now bought the Spar shop that replaced SCATS. Fortunately for the local community and the town's character, many small independent shops remain.*

The Square

St Georges Square, which used to be the focal point of the town, is now normally known as The Square.

It contains several Georgian facaded buildings including Austin & Wyatt, Barclays Bank, and the Golden Boat Chinese restaurant (formerly the Kings Head Inn). Markets had been held in Bishop's Waltham since the reign of King Edward 1 (1272-1307) and a market house erected in the early 1700s used to stand in the centre of The Square; it was used as a jail for French prisoners during the Napoleonic Wars and was demolished in 1841. Occasional street markets have been reintroduced in recent years, based in The Square and High Street, and on themes such as local farmers' produce and French food.

Top: The west side of The Square in June 1966, before the construction of Driver's solicitors offices in the gap to the right of Austin & Wyatt's. The Square was on the main east-west traffic route through the town, and the No.51 bus is passing through on its way to Swanmore. The house in the centre was the home of the Padwick family until it was pulled down to make way for the new road around the back of The Crown.

Bottom: The 2011 view shows that the Padwicks' house has been demolished and replaced by a bus shelter, beyond which is a small open space, the overall effect being to remove The Square's sense of enclosure. A new building of architectural merit and sensitivity is required to enclose The Square again. The red telephone box, based on a much loved design by the architect Sir Giles Gilbert Scott, was moved eastwards when Driver's offices were built.

For comparative views of The Square from the west, see page 59.

Top: *A fine picture of the south-east part of The Square in the early 1920s, a traffic-free scene. In the background is The Crown Hotel, offering luncheons and teas, and displaying one of the AA signs that used to be so familiar.*

The older part of The Crown dates from the 16th century; the part with the single gable was built c1900 to house a public bar with clubroom above. The Crown was once a coaching inn with two courtyards at the rear surrounded by stables and other buildings that were demolished to make way for the new bypass.

The attractive building to the right with three jettied gables was a butchers shop for more than a century. Beyond the road signpost is the wall and well-treed garden of Eastway, a large house.

Centre: *The Crown Hotel c1960, when Strong & Co. of Romsey were the brewery. The Women's Institute market used the building to the right for many years.*

Bottom: *The Crown is unoccupied and awaiting restoration and refurbishment by the new owners, Fullers, who intend to re-open it early in 2012. On the front of the old butchers shop, recently an estate agents, is the name of Walter West, butchers who occupied the premises for decades, in the glazed tiles below the shop window. To the left of the picture are houses on the Eastways estate, built on the site of Eastway c1970.*

Facing page top left: The south-west corner of The Square in 1968, when the foundations of Driver's offices were being laid. The houses and buildings beyond the workmen, as well as the Padwicks' house on the right, were all subsequently demolished to allow for the bypass.

Facing page bottom left: In the 2011 view the island has been moved southwards and the road signs have been replaced by the Millennium Clock which was installed in 2002.

Facing page top right: Churcher's shop (house furnisher and dealer in antiques) for sale in 1961.

Facing page bottom right: It was replaced by the extension to Lloyds Bank, seen in the 2011 view, a modern utilitarian building. Gone too are the splendidly balustraded steps up to the front of what is now the Golden Boat Chinese restaurant. At the time it was the offices of Frank Stubbs, sales agents for Churcher's property. (See also page 39).

Top: Taken in September 1968, looking north along Coal Yard Lane towards The Square.

Bottom: The only reference points in the 2011 picture are the end of the Driver Belcher's building on the right and the white walled building at the rear of Barclays Bank, beyond. All the buildings in Coal Yard Lane, and Northy's coal yard to which it led, were demolished soon after the 1968 picture was taken, to make way for the new bypass.

Brook Street

Brook Street gets its name from the brook known as the Lord's River (which surrounded the outer court of the Palace), which used to be an open stream until culverted. As is evident from the two pairs of pictures on this page, the southern part of Brook Street has been widened, old buildings on the west side demolished, and much of its character lost.

Top left: A view taken in the early 1900s of Brook Street from The Square. The street and wisteria-covered Brook Cottage made an attractive view until the buildings were demolished in 1973.

Bottom left: The new houses were set back to widen the road and provide a pavement. On the right are service buildings of St George's House, now part of Barclays Bank, and home to the Bishop's Waltham Museum from 1987 for about 20 years.

Top right: Brook Street, in the early 1900s, looking towards The Square. The old warehouses and bakehouse on the right were demolished in 1973 for new housing accompanied by road widening. On the left are the backs of High Street properties, including The Merchants House.

Bottom right: The view in 2011 illustrates the effects of road widening and the intrusion of parked cars and waste bins.

Facing page top left: Cross Street was very narrow, and in 1917 the splendid old timber building and blacksmiths forge on the corner of Brook Street had to be demolished because it was so badly damaged by a lorry.

Facing page bottom left: The building that now occupies the site is used by Penyards, estate agents.

Facing page top right: The northern part of Brook Street c1900. The office on the right is that of Arthur Davis's mineral water works and he is pictured standing outside with his daughters. Next door George Eldridge stands outside the Brewery Tap public house. The buildings beyond, jutting forward slightly, belong to the mineral water works. In the distance, beyond the horse and cart, is the Brewery Arms on the corner of Bank Street and Lower Lane.

Facing page bottom right: In 2011 this row of buildings is still recognisable, although the office has become a private house and the Brewery Tap is now used partly by the Citizens Advice Bureau and a betting shop. The old mineral water works buildings are now occupied by Malt House Studios.

Lower Lane

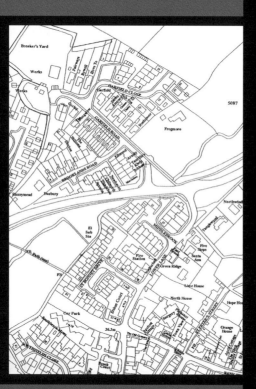

Far left: The 25" map (1870s) shows Lower Lane heading north from the town centre. Already a route by the late medieval period, it was originally known as North Brook Lane after the stream running parallel to the west. The road connecting Lower Lane to the Gas Works became known as Garfield Road. Just south of the junction with Garfield Road, the house known as Frogmore became Middlebrook. On the same side of the road, but further south, is Edwards & Sons' Brewery, built in the 1890s although brewing ceased in the 1920s. Opposite is the Independent Chapel, built in 1862, which became the Congregational Church, and later the United Reformed Church; it was demolished in 1979.

Left: The 2001 version of the 1/2500 scale map shows significant changes. The new road along the west side of the North Pond sweeps round and the junctions with Garfield Road and Lower Lane have been staggered. There are housing estates both sides of Garfield Road, and the old Gas Works is now a car breakers yard. The house Middlebrook was demolished in 1969 to make way for the small housing estate with the same name. On the site of The Brewery, which was subsequently occupied by Duke's Brewery Mill, a housing estate (St Bonnet Drive) has been built. The United Reformed Church and adjoining cottages have been demolished to make way for the present doctors' surgery.

Facing page top left: In this pre-1969 view looking south along Lower Lane, the junction with Garfield Road is on the right, and the house in the centre is Middlebrook. In the murky distance the Brewery Mill buildings can just about be seen.

Facing page bottom left: The Middlebrook housing estate occupies the site of the house, and the junction with Garfield Road has disappeared.

Facing page top right: The Corhampton Road section of the town centre bypass, under construction, is seen from one of the houses being built at Middlebrook. Garfield Road, lined with old terraced houses facing modern bungalows, is in the upper part of the picture. In the distance is the old gas holder.

Facing page bottom right: As the view from the same spot in 2011 is obscured by trees, the modern view is taken from further east, looking up Garfield Road. New houses have been built on the left.

Top: *Brewery Mill in April 1969 on the site of Edwards' brewery, which had been taken over by Dukes in the 1930s. Duke's used the buildings as a processing plant for animal feedstuffs. On the right is the front façade of the Congregational Church.*

Bottom: *By 2011 the site had been redeveloped for housing, the flats along the street frontage being appropriately named Dukes Court. The houses of St.Bonnet Drive occupy the rest of the site of the former Brewery Mill.*

Facing page top left: *Portland Square, looking towards Bank Street in 1962. This scene illustrates the run-down nature of parts of Bishop's Waltham in the early 1960s. The buildings on the right belonged to the old school, which was once the Bishop's Waltham Grammar School, founded in 1679, though it is thought that the original school may have been in Southbrook House next door (fronting Brook Street).*

Facing page bottom left: *Soon after the 1962 picture was taken, the old school buildings were demolished to make way for the Lower Lane car park.*

Facing page top right: *The view westwards from the western end of Bank Street (probably taken in the early 1960s) shows the junction with Brook Street to the left and Lower Lane to the right. On the far left is part of the old Granary. In the centre, facing up Bank Street, is a shop and cottage. The road sign on the cottage indicates the way to Corhampton for traffic emerging from the town centre.*

Facing page bottom right: *In the 2011 view the buildings on the left and right of the earlier photo still exist, but the cottage and shop (along with the remains of the old Grammar School behind) have been demolished, and the site forms part of the Lower Lane car park.*

Bank Street West

Right top: *This view of Bank Street from the junction with Lower Lane and Brook Street is dominated by the old Granary on the right. This was owned for many years by Duke's, who also owned Brewery Mill nearby and Abbey Mill in Station Road. On the left side of Bank Street is Gable House, seen from the west.*

Right bottom: *The tallest part of the Granary building has been a Crafts Centre since the mid-1970s and the lower part to the right is Banks Bar Bistro. The façade of Vine Cottage, the house beyond the Granary, has been markedly improved. The patch of land on the left, on which the white van is parked in the earlier photo, is now a small amenity area where people relax on their way in or out of the town centre.*

Below left: *Gable House in Bank Street, c1912. The Victorian red brick frontage conceals the remains of a medieval hall house, dating from 1430. It is one of the oldest buildings in Bishop's Waltham.*

To the west of Gable House stood Henry Southwell's shed (he was a wheelwright and coachbuilder) and The Brewery Arms, which was on the corner of Lower Lane; this became a butchers shop.

Below right: *In the 2011 view, Gable House has changed little. However, Southwell's shed and The Brewery Arms have been demolished, the latter to widen the road junction.*

Left top: The north side of Bank Street, from the top of the High Street, in April 1973, with Askew's shop on the corner of St Peter's Street. The shop had been for many years a general store and is in an ancient building, dating possibly from the 15th century and certainly from the early 1500s. The adjoining building to the right was a bakehouse.

Left bottom: The scene in 2011 is much the same, except that Askew's shop closed in 1984 and is now a dwelling.

Below left: The view eastwards along Bank Street from the High Street, in May 1968. The first house on the left is Town View, a timber-framed building with a Georgian facade, which was a doctor's house and surgery (the surgery was replaced by the one in Lower Lane in 1979). The grey rendered house next door, St Peter's House, once housed the Bishop's Waltham Telephone Exchange (the cottage at the rear, fronting St Peter's Street, is called Exchange Cottage).

Below right: In the 2011 view the shop on the corner of the High Street, although it has changed hands several times, is once again a sweet shop! The square building beyond on the corner of Houchin Street was demolished in 1973 for road widening and redevelopment, and is now a building of character containing the Anvil Tea Rooms.

Houchin Street

Houchin Street was a narrow back street until the 1960s, then many houses on the east side (some were ancient timber-framed buildings) were demolished to make way for a new car park in the centre of the town and the road was also widened to facilitate the flow of traffic. As a result, it was no longer an interesting street, but became more of a service road.

These changes are also evident when comparing the aerial photos on page 18.

Top: This view of the top end of Houchin Street, taken c1962, shows some of the old cottages that were pulled down for the new car park. Beyond the milk float is Askew's shop on Bank Steet.

Bottom: The 2011 scene is of a wider road, a car parking area, and some new buildings towards Bank Street, including the premises occupied by Pat Staples, interior designer, until 2010. A new Italian restaurant, Piccola Roma, is planning to open there at the end of 2011 . As in so many modern streets, waste bins detract from the street scene.

Red Lion Street, earlier known as Middle Street, connected Houchin Street to Basingwell Street and the High Street. It was renamed after a public house which stood approximately where the pedestrian way now crosses the car park.

Top left: When this view was taken in January 1972, Richards' ironmongery shop still stood on the corner of Houchin Street and Red Lion Street. The Primitive Methodist (now United Free) Church (St Pauls) on Basingwell Street can be seen in the distance.

The demolition of the shop for the car park later that year caused considerable argument. Such controversies ultimately changed national planning policy more in favour of conservation than demolition of locally important old buildings.

Bottom left: The equivalent view today is much less interesting. Richards' shop was where the bicycle stands are now.

Above: The Red Lion public house being demolished in February 1966, its ancient

Top: *Looking south down Houchin Street towards The Crown Inn in July 1961. Red Lion Street crosses the street in the foreground. Beyond, on the left, is Richards' ironmongery shop and terraces of cottages opening direct on to the narrow pavement. On the opposite side of the narrow street are the backs of High Street properties.*

Bottom: *The most notable change is the disappearance of Richards' shop and the cottages, replaced by car parking with easy access to the High Street. The planners also took the opportunity to widen this section of Houchin Street. Still recognisable from the foreground of the 1961 scene are the Bishop's Waltham Social Club building on the left, and the old building on the right with the hipped gable roof occupied by Annabel's dress shop until mid 2011.*

Facing page top left: *Houchin Street looking north from near The Square in the 1950s, with the rear part of the SCATS (Southern Counties Agricultural Trading Society) shop on the left, and the tall building at the rear of the Post Office. The ground floor of this building was the sorting office and the upper floor was later used by the Bishop's Waltham Glass company. On the right are cottages that had become used for storage by SCATS.*

Facing page bottom left: *In the 2011 view the SCATS building is still in use but by the Co-op. The tall building remains, although the upper part had been reconstructed; the rear of the ground floor is occupied by Country Attics. The cottages on the right have been converted into offices (Merlin Mews).*

Facing page top right: *This photograph of Frank Stubbs' estate agency on the corner of The Square and Houchin Street, was taken in March 1973. The building, which was formerly the Kings Head public house, dates from the 18th century. Buildings at the rear included the pub's stable block. The pub closed prior to the First World War. On the left is the pair of cottages in which Matthews' shop was situated, which closed in 1983.*

Facing page bottom right: *By 2011 the former Kings Head had become a Chinese restaurant, Golden Boat R2, and Matthews' shop is now partly a private residence whilst behind the bay window is the optometrists Fithyan & Saxby.*

Basingwell Street

Basingwell Street was Basselwell Street in medieval times, possibly derived from the well or spring that issued there.

Top: Upper Basingwell Street, looking towards Bank Street, c1914, completely devoid of traffic. On the left is the community pump which served the area for many years, until around 1932.

Bottom: In the 2011 view the street scene is dominated by parked vehicles. Although the cottages on the right still stand, those on the left have been demolished for the central car park. A replica of the community pump has been installed by the Bishop's Waltham Society in the vicinity of the original.

Facing page top left: Children pose outside the slaughterhouse in Basingwell Street, c1905. Just beyond them is the 18th century barn and yard used for many years by Hale Brothers, who in the 1890s built some important buildings in Bishop's Waltham including the Institute in Bank Street and the Oddfellows Hall in High Street.

Facing page bottom left: The brick wall on the left still remains and encloses a courtyard for the offices of Giles Wheeler-Bennett, chartered surveyors, but the barn and yard beyond have been replaced by Basing Mews housing development. Most of the cottages on the right in the 1905 view still stand, although two were demolished so that St Paul's Church (which opened in 1910) could be built.

Facing page top right: The Barleycorn Inn in the 1920s, with landlord Edwin Ward and his grand-daughter standing on the steps. The sign shows that the Inn served beer brewed by Edwards' Brewery in Lower Lane; previously the brewers had been Eldridge Pope of Dorchester. The building, which dates from the 17th century and is oak-beamed, was the Parish Workhouse from 1762 to around 1808 (for a while Basingwell Street even became known as Workhouse Street). The building has been an inn since the late 1800s.

Facing page bottom right: The modern view is remarkably similar.

Little Shore Lane

Until the 1950s Little Shore Lane was a country lane running eastwards from the historic core of Bishop's Waltham to Mount Farm and the fields beyond.

Top: St Paul's Church was built as a Primitive Methodist Church in 1910 on the site of old cottages, at a cost of £672, with money raised by members. It is now the United Free Church.

Bottom left: The view from Basingwell Street along Little Shore Lane, in 1962. On the left is the United Free Church.

Bottom right: As can be seen in the modern shot, the nearer of the two timber-clad buildings on the right has been converted to residential use, the other has been demolished.

Facing page top left: Looking west along Little Shore Lane towards Basingwell Street, c1964.

Facing page bottom left: The view in 2011 is very similar. The single-storey gabled building on the left, once a chapel of rest, is now occupied by a small electrical services company, and part of the wall to the left has been demolished to provide access to the St John's Ambulance building. Behind the trees on the right is Malvern Close, where there was a field in 1964.

Facing page top right: The eastern end of Little Shore Lane with Mount House and its adjoining barn, in February 1962.

Facin page bottom right: The modern view shows that both Mount House and the barn have been demolished and replaced by new houses. The wall on the right remains, and is now on the frontage of the Jubilee Hall. Ken Wright and Val Harfield take a rest after shopping.

Claylands

In the mid-19th century a terracotta works was opened to the west of the town, which led to the development of the suburb of Newtown. The first company (The Clay Company) failed in 1867 but in 1871 the works were taken over by another company (M.H. Blanchard & Co.) that produced bricks and tiles as well. The company was owned by the Blanchards, a philanthropic family who built decent homes for their workers. The Brick and Tile Works became one of the most important in Hampshire. Its products were used in Buckingham Palace and the Victoria & Albert Museum in London, and were also exported to many parts of the world. It closed in 1957.

Photographed by Paul Desa, Bishop's Waltham.

MESSRS. M. H. BLANCHARD & CO.'S WORKS.

Top: The main Works viewed from Winchester Road, c1906, with the rim of the clay pit on the left behind Claylands House (see page 45). The fields in the foreground have been built on.

Bottom left: The 1910 6" map shows the Works situated at the northern end of Claylands Road, with the clay pits beyond. The coming of the railway in the 1860s had been important for the expansion of the Works, which the map shows connected to the Bishop's Waltham branch by a single track line from the vicinity of the Station, across the fields of Pondside Farm. The developments along the Winchester Road, Victoria Road, Avenue Road (as it was then called) and Park Road comprise mainly the houses that were built in the second half of the 19th century to house the workers at the Brick and Tile Works.

Bottom right: The 2001 1/10000 scale map shows the major changes that have occurred in the area. The Works buildings have all gone (with minor exceptions), as has the railway connection, although part of its route is discernable.

Some of the Works site and buildings were used initially for Civil Defence training, and later by the Ambulance Service. Today the Works site is mainly a large industrial estate, and Claylands Road has been extended and widened to provide access for large vehicles.

The old clay pits are now a Nature Reserve (see page 46). Between Claylands Road and the town centre, extensive housing development (mainly the Pondside estate on the fields of Pondside Farm) has taken place, served primarily by the section of town centre bypass that was built along the old railway line.

Above: A group of workmen around a kiln at the Newtown Works, in the early 1900s. At its peak in the 1890s the Works employed around 200 men.

Top right: Claylands House in 1968. It had been built around 1880 by the Works proprietor, Mark Henry Blanchard senior, as a family home and showpiece of the products manufactured by the Newtown Works. It was a fine building in red and blue brickwork with terracotta ornamentation. The demolition of Claylands House in 1974 was very regrettable, and would surely not have been allowed in more enlightened times.

Bottom right: The site is now occupied by Council houses, and there are light industrial sites further along Claylands Road.

Claylands Nature Reserve

After closure of the Brick & Tile Works in the 1950s, the old clay pit in Claylands Road became overgrown. The warm south-facing slopes of the pit became important for wildflowers and insects, especially butterflies - 28 species have been recorded. Small ponds provide homes for all three species of British newts. The area was later designated as a Site of Importance for Nature Conservation.

In the late 1980s Hampshire County Council acquired the site. Since 1990 HCC's Countryside Service has managed it as a Local Nature Reserve, later extended to include the bottom meadow (between the Recycling Centre and the slopes of the old pit) and Harvey's Meadows to the north. Eighteen ponds have been created in the Reserve, harbouring the rare and legally protected Great Crested Newt.

There has been extensive community involvement at Claylands, from local fundraising to assist with the acquisition and management of the Nature Reserve (Friends of Waltham's Wildlife have been very supportive), to volunteers helping the Senior Ranger, Peter Potts, with practical conservation tasks on site. Claylands Nature Reserve is now a great local asset enjoyed by the community.

Top right: The top of the slope provides a good view over Bishop's Waltham. Old Winchester Hill is visible on a clear day. In the foreground is the bottom meadow.

Bottom right: Youngsters from the nearby Battery Hill estate are assisting with the construction of steps, in 1995.

Below left: A Great Crested Newt being handled (under licence from English Nature!) by the late Martin Eustace. Each newt has its own pattern of markings, just like every human being has a unique fingerprint.

Below right: Butterfly monitoring has been carried out at Claylands for the past 20 years, and the site is notable in particular for the Marbled White.

Nature Notes

NEW ACCESS FACILITIES AT THE CLAYLANDS NATURE RESERVE, BISHOPS WALTHAM

Hampshire County Council's, Countryside & Community Department's Countryside Service have started a project to improve access facilities to its Claylands Local Nature Reserve in Bishops Waltham.

The project is being jointly run by rangers from the County's Countryside Service based at Titchfield Haven Nature Reserve and by the Bishops Waltham Branch of Hampshire Wildlife Trust. Claylands Nature Reserve is a small site at the end of Claylands Rd, which comprises the banks of the old claypit. The site is a much cherished local asset used by local residents for quiet walks around the rural fringe of the village. The site is a valuable nature conservation site with many species of interesting plants and butterflies.

Following works last summer to formalise the access arrangements, when the Countryside Service put in five stiles and special dog stiles, a second phase of works has begun. A start has been made on surfacing some of the well used

in July when Hampshire Conservation Volunteers stayed in Bishops Waltham for the week-end and worked alongside the Countryside Ranger Peter Potts, who is responsible for looking after the site. The volunteers were

Country Corner

Hampshire land owners have warned that government plans to extend the 'right to buy' to tenants of housing associations could undermine the whole philosophy of providing village homes for village people. The warning from the Country Landowners' Association (CLA), follows the publication of the government's white paper "Our Future Homes" which contains proposals to extend the right to buy to social tenants, people in low-cost housing schemes or those sharing ownerships of their home with a housing association. In conjunction with the Joseph Rowntree Foundation the CLA recently carried out a major survey into rented housing in rural area and as a result believes that such a move would be mistaken. Land owners believe it is essential that social housing schemes in rural areas remain available and accessible to local families on a rented or shared ownership basis. It is their feeling that when people living in affordable housing schemes want to become outright owners of their own homes that they should be encouraged to buy homes on the open market with grant support from the governments existing tenants' incentive scheme. In order that village families should be able to remain in village communities it is essential that a pool of social housing should be maintained which will be available for future generations.

Local youngsters - Jamie, Mike and Richard Manby, Russell Lambeth and Neil Cole.

Newtown

The suburb of Newtown developed in the second half of the 19th century to the west of the town centre in response to the need to provide houses, a school, pub and other facilities for the brick and tile works employees and their families. Most of the buildings from the period survive, and give a distinctive character to this part of Bishop's Waltham.

Top left: Victoria Buildings in 1909, a row of red-bricked terraced houses that had been built in 1863 at the junction of Victoria Road and Winchester Road.

Bottom left: More than a century later the scene has changed little, except for the insertion of modern windows.

Below: Marks Terrace fronting Winchester Road just west of the junction with Claylands Road. Marks Terrace was built in 1901 for brickyard workmen, and was named after Mark Henry Blanchard senior, proprietor until he died in 1892.

Top: *The Railway Inn, c1912. The landlord was James Sanger, whose family also ran a local coal merchants business. Two of their carts can be seen, the one in front of the pub loaded with sacks of coal. The public house was probably built in the early 1860s to serve the workmen from the newly formed Bishop's Waltham Clay Company. On the right is Victoria Road, and in the distance can be seen the distinctive gables of Newtown School, "the school on the hill".*

Centre: *The same view, probably in the early 1960s. By then the front of the Railway Inn looked much more modern, and Brickwoods were the brewers. Beer was available by the bottle or jug to take away. On the extreme right of the picture can be seen part of the Territorial Army's Drill Hall, built in 1914.*

Bottom: *By 2011 the pub had become the Priory Inn, still a popular pub serving the local community. The school has been converted to flats, with a new block of flats alongside, well designed in harmony with the old school.*

Facing page top left: *Shows the terrace of six cottages built at the western end of Victoria Road c1910, soon after they had been built.*

Facing page bottom left: *In 2011 the cottages look much the same as they did 100 years ago, except for some of the windows. Just beyond the left end of the terrace there is now a small group of flats (Victoria Flats), built on the site of a builders yard in the early 1990s. The archway, seen in the earlier picture, which connected the later Victoria Buildings to the 1863 terrace featured on the previous page, was knocked down by a lorry about 1940.*

Facing page top right: *The terraces of Victoria Buildings still thrive. By contrast, Albert Terrace has not survived. The tall terrace of houses on the south side of Winchester Road is shown in September 1973 in the process of demolition.*

Facing page bottom right: *It was replaced by Priory Court, an old people's home.*

Newtown School

The school was built in 1865, on the corner of Victoria Road and Albert Road, with provision for 200 children and a master's residence. It was enlarged in 1894/5 to take 300 children.

Top left: *The school in the late 1800s with young pupils standing outside.*

Bottom left: *By the 1980s the School had become redundant and the main building was converted into flats, carefully retaining the appearance of the 1865 building. To the right of the old school building can be seen one of the small blocks of flats built in the school grounds as "enabling development" to finance the sensitive conversion of the old building to residential use.*

Below: *Pupils in the classroom at Newtown School in 1927.*

The Priory

The Priory has an interesting history. It was the brainchild of Arthur Helps, the man who first developed the Claylands brick works and who was instrumental in bringing the railway to Bishop's Waltham (see page 7). The town needed its own hospital and, because of his political and royal connections, Helps enlisted the support of Queen Victoria for the building of what was to be called the Royal Albert Infirmary. Enough sponsorship was raised to build it, and in 1864 the foundation stone was laid by Prince Leopold, the Queen's 11-year-old son. However, the Infirmary never opened because insufficient funds were raised to actually run it.

In 1875 it was auctioned, with 11 acres of land, for £500 and became a private house, later called The Priory (the name stuck!). It was subsequently bought by the White Fathers African Missionary Society and used as the headquarters of this Roman Catholic organisation from 1911 until 1967. It was then acquired by Hampshire County Council and used as a Police Training School from 1972 until 1988, when it became disused.

Although a building of some historic and architectural interest, it was demolished in 1993 and 42 houses built on the immediate site of the buildings (Elizabeth Way). The surrounding land was bought by the Parish Council to provide a large open space (Priory Park).

Top: *The Priory in 1908 when it was a private house.*

Centre: *When this view was taken in 1962, The Priory was the headquarters of the White Fathers, a boarding school for Catholic boys.*

Bottom: *This view taken from the old railway line in March 1975 shows the Priory (on the right) when it was at its peak as a Police Training College, having been substantially extended.*

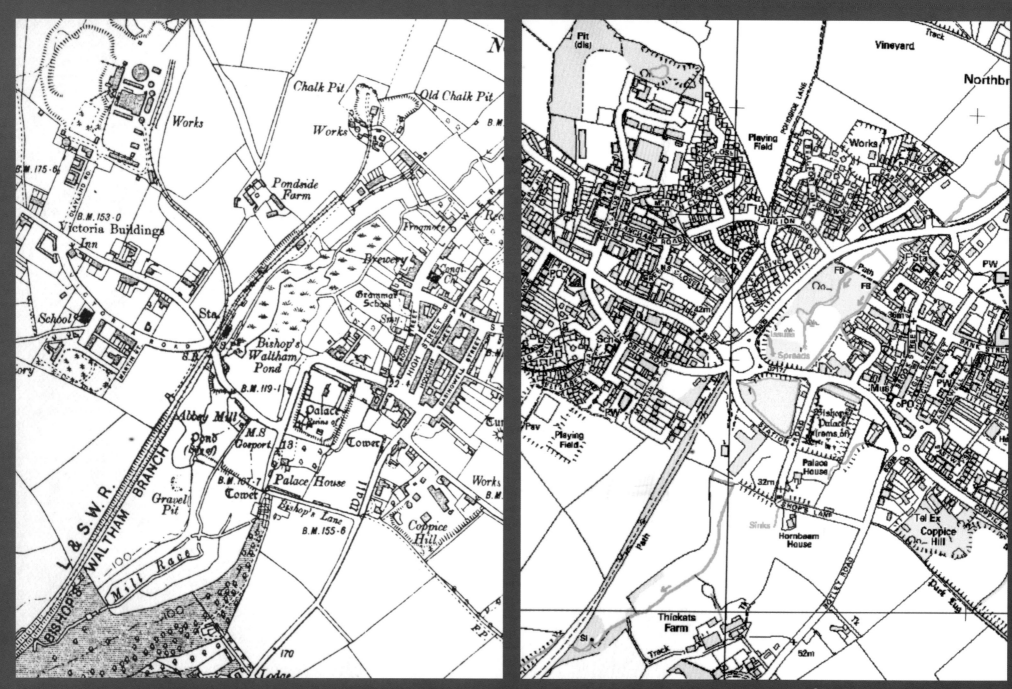

The Railway

The Railway came to Bishop's Waltham as a single track branch line from Botley, in 1863. Originally it had been planned to carry the line beyond Bishop's Waltham to Brockbridge, near Droxford, then north along the route that later became the Meon Valley line to Alton and, eventually, London. However, the section to Brockbridge was never built. Although beneficial to the town because it connected it to the national railway network, the branch line was never very successful in economic terms. It closed to passenger traffic as early as 1933, and to freight traffic in 1962; thus the line did not quite reach its centenary.

Facing page left: The 1910 6" map shows the Bishop's Waltham branch, part of the LSWR (London & South Western Railway) network, coming from the Botley direction to a terminus station by the junction of Winchester, Victoria and Station Roads. The line continues beyond the Station to a goods yard, with a single track continuing to the chalk pits where the town's gas works had been built. Another single track went from the Station in a north-west direction to the Brick & Tile Works at Claylands, Newtown.

Facing page right: On the 2001 version of the 1/10000 map the main evidence that a railway ever existed is the old trackbed, running south-west from the site of the former Station (now a large roundabout), along which runs a footpath. Careful scrutiny of the routes of the sidings to the old gas works and the Claylands works shows that some boundaries of post-war housing developments align with short sections of trackbed.

Top: Bishop's Waltham Station, probably soon after the introduction of the steam railmotor service in 1904; Railmotor No.1 is in the platform. The Station was unusually attractive for a small branch line terminus, as it was built of bricks and tiles from the local Claylands Works. The station house features a mixture of red and yellow bricks, and the chimneys display brickwork in horizontal and chevron patterns. (Source: National Railway Museum)

Bottom: In this scene dating from around 1905, horse drawn vehicles wait outside the Station to carry passengers to their destination. On the left is Sid Rogers with his carriage for passengers, and on the right is Harry Fielder who would have carried the luggage. Travel posters on the Station wall advertise the attractions of far away places such as Bideford, in north Devon.

Railway Station, Bishops Waltham, Hants.   5294.

Facing page top left: The Railway Station viewed from Victoria Road, c1920. Even then, the roof is showing signs of neglect. The road from the town centre comes in from the right, across the level crossing, and towards Upham and Winchester to the left. Beyond the typically LSWR 'Bishop's Waltham' station sign are the trees lining the west bank of the Great Pond.

Facing page bottom left: The same view is very different in 2011. When the town centre bypass was constructed, the large roundabout at the junction of the two sections (now the B3035 and B2177) was created on the site of the old Station. To the left of the picture, a recent housing development (Pilgrims Gate) has been built at the junction of Victoria and Winchester Roads.

Facing page top right: The view along the goods yard from the Station, with the goods shed on the right. In the centre is the water tank used for replenishing steam locomotives. The line to the left of the wagons goes to the Works at Claylands. Over the field to the left is Pondside Farmhouse.

Facing page bottom right: The trackbed is now occupied by the B3035 road to Corhampton. The layby on the right is roughly where the goods shed used to be. A magnificent stand of trees has grown along the left side of the road, screening the houses of the Pondside estate beyond.

The Bishop's Waltham Railway Path

After the branch line was closed, Hampshire County Council acquired the trackbed from the old Station to the parish boundary, with the intention of providing a new road to link the Botley Road to the town. However, this never materialised, and the old trackbed remained derelict and overgrown for many years. In 1987, members of the Bishop's Waltham Society persuaded the County Council to turn it into a footpath, so that people could walk direct from the town into the open countryside to the south. The Society created an appropriate entrance to the path by installing level crossing gates (not the originals; they were too far gone) and a section of track, as well as two display panels illustrating the history of the locality. The Path now forms part of the Hampshire Millennium Pilgrims' Trail (from Winchester to Caen via Portsmouth and Cherbourg), and the first section from the roundabout to Brooklands Farm is managed by the County Council as a local nature reserve.

Top: The northern end of the derelict railway line in April 1984.

Bottom: The later view shows the inviting entrance to the Railway Path created by the Bishop's Waltham Society in 1987.

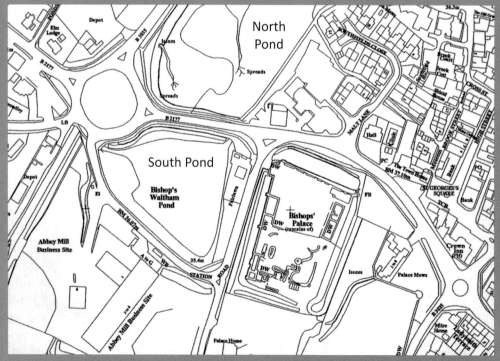

Town Centre Bypass

Until the late 1960s, traffic travelling from Winchester to Botley or Wickham and Fareham would have had to pass through the centre of Bishop's Waltham.

As the First Edition OS map (1870) shows, the Winchester Road from the west crossed the Bishop's Waltham branch line at a level crossing by the Station, then went around the southern edge of the medieval Bishop's Waltham Pond, and the west and north sides of the Palace ruins. The road continued along Station Road and through St George's Square then, having taken a right-angled turn at the end of The Crown Inn, emerged from the Square to the junction of the roads to Botley and Wickham. This was at an angled T-junction with the Wickham traffic having priority.

The later map (2001) shows that, following closure of the railway, the opportunity was taken to construct a town centre bypass to relieve The Square of the increasing numbers of cars and lorries passing through it. The Station building was demolished and a large roundabout constructed on the site. From the roundabout a new road was constructed across the Pond, dividing it into two (now known as the North and South Ponds) and removing traffic from the road past Abbey Mill and the west side of the Palace. This remnant of Station Road has become a little-used lane.

Alongside the north wall of the Palace the new road followed approximately the alignment of the old, but was widened substantially. This involved the demolition of what had once been the outer courtyard of the Palace, including the former Palace stables. From the north-east corner of the Palace, the new road was set on a direct course to the junction of the roads to Botley and Wickham. As part of the scheme, virtually all of the buildings fronting the section of Station Road leading into the Square were demolished. The new road severed Coal Yard Lane that had led from The Square to the coal yard by the Palace wall. It also passed through the courtyards at the rear of The Crown. A new crossroads was constructed south of the Crown to form a new junction between the bypass and the roads from the town centre, Botley and Wickham.

Top: *First Edition OS map (1870).*

Bottom: *2001 map.*

Top: *The view eastwards from the front of the Station in 1965. Brushwood foundations are being laid for the causeway across the Pond. To the right the Palace ruins can be seen across what would become the South Pond, before it was restored from its silted-up state in the 1970s.*

Using brushwood as a foundation for roads that cross marshy ground was a technique apparently used by Iron Age Britons (so recent research shows) and was frequently used by the Romans. It was revived as a technique in the mid 18th century when new road building became an economic necessity right across Britain.

It is a testament to its strength and longevity that few drivers realise that, using the road today, they are driving along a road with 45 year-old brushwood foundations taking both much heavier lorries and many more cars than would have been the case when it was first built. It is said that if you stand on the road between the ponds you can feel some movement when heavy goods vehicles pass but that is possibly a matter of personal opinion!

Bottom: *From the same viewpoint in 2011. The photographer is standing on the large roundabout that was built on the Station site. The road signs direct traffic along the bypass towards Wickham and Botley. On the right a thick screen of trees now hides the South Pond and the Palace.*

Facing page top left: *Looking along Station Road towards the town centre from the north-west corner of the Palace in February 1962. On the right is the brick wall around the Palace grounds, and on the left are the former Palace stables. Beyond the house fronting Station Road are the low wall and garden trees of a house called The Elms. Further on is the Star Garage, occupying the space now used by Fox's Garden Machinery. In the distance is Lloyds Bank, in St George's Square.*

Facing page bottom left: *The town centre bypass, looking east. On the left is the tall brick wall of Budgens supermarket, and beyond is the disused Youth Hall. To the right of the white-walled building, Lloyds Bank can be glimpsed.*

Facing page top right: *The view west along Station Road in February 1962 with the former Palace stables on the right. Beyond are the old Youth Hall (in a former Salvation Army 'citadel') and the premises of Glider Coaches, with Southwell's Garage visible beyond the petrol pumps. The only car is a Ford Anglia, about to negotiate the left bend around the Palace grounds.*

Facing page bottom right: *Budgens supermarket now dominates the similar view. Part of the Glider site is still a filling station. To the right of Budgens is Malt Lane (moved further to the west as part of the new layout) leading to Southfields Close.*

Top: *The east end of Station Road, looking towards St George's Square, c1968. On the right is the Fire Station building, and the single storey building further along, with the sign outside, was the Pennyfarthing Café. On the left is the low wall of The Elms, or Elms House, once the home of the Rooke family who ran the garage further along the road.*

Bottom: *Lloyds Bank in The Square is the only recognisable feature from the same viewpoint today. The buildings in Station Road have been demolished, and replaced by a patch of grass, a bus shelter, bins and signs. The tarmacked footpath to the Square is almost the only reminder of the original line of the road although the sign, just visible on the wall of Town House, still says Station Road. To the right the bypass sweeps round to the junction with the roads to Botley and Wickham.*

Facing page top left: In July 1968 the roads from Botley (left) and Wickham (right) converge before entering The Square past the Crown Inn. Across the centre of the picture are buildings of the former courtyard of The Crown; by the late 1960s many of the buildings were semi-derelict.

Facing page bottom left: It is impossible to use the same viewpoint now, as houses have been built on the grassy area in the foreground of the old photo. The buildings of the east wing of The Crown are still recognisable, albeit with more windows. The courtyard buildings have been demolished for the bypass, which now joins the roads from the town centre, Botley and Wickham at a roundabout

Facing page top right: The view from the foot of Crown Hill (the road from Botley) towards The Crown Inn. On the left are the buildings at the rear of The Crown, and on the right is the corner of a building in what was Lidlow's builders' yard.

Facing page bottom right: The main point of reference today is the gabled end of the east wing of The Crown. However, the attractive rear elevation of the historic main range of The Crown's buildings is now more visible. The awkward junction of the Botley and Wickham roads has been replaced by a roundabout, and the town centre bypass joins from the left.

Top: The rear of the Crown Inn in September 1968, with the stables partially demolished in preparation for the construction of the new road. Reputedly, in the early part of the 19th century, Bishop's Waltham was known as a great place for cock-fighting which took place in "a barn close to The Crown Inn" which drew many 'sporting men' into the town. It is possible the building being demolished was the barn in question.

Bottom: A group known as the Crown Inn Minstrels photographed at the back of The Crown in 1900.

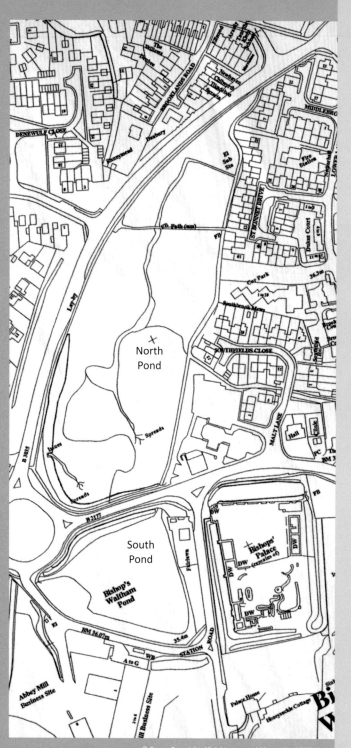

Scheduled Ancient Monument

Bishop's Waltham Palace is classified by English Heritage as a "Magnate's Residence".

A medieval magnate's residence is defined as "a very high-status residence of domestic rather than military character. Such residences were the palaces or houses of royalty, bishops and the highest rank of nobility who were usually closely linked to the monarch".

There are only 150 Magnate's Residences in the country and thus this is a relatively rare type of archaeological site. The Palace itself is in the Guardianship of the State and is cared for by English Heritage. The Palace, South Pond and, south of Station Road, Abbey Field (the eastern side of the old pond clearly visible in the 1909 map), are all part of a Scheduled Ancient Monument - the highest level of protection there is.

Left: 1909 version of 25" map.

Right: 2001 version of 1/2500 map.

The Ponds

The medieval Bishops of Winchester lived in fine style, befitting their rank and wealth. For the banquets that they laid on for their guests, fresh fish were required to be available. The bishops created several fish ponds, including those at Frensham, Alresford and Bishop's Waltham.

Bishop Henry de Blois created two fish ponds to the west of Bishop's Waltham Palace by damming the River Hamble. The dam for the Great Pond was used to carry the road from the west side of Bishop's Waltham into the town. This road, later known as Station Road, still skirts the southern side of what is now the South Pond, passing in front of the former Abbey Mill. The Great Pond used to extend half a mile upstream to Northbrook, but after the destruction of the Palace the Pond gradually silted up.

The smaller pond lay to the south of the Great Pond but had been drained by the middle of the 19th century. During the latter part of the 20th century the site was partly developed as an industrial estate, and is the location of Sainsbury's proposed superstore. The dam still survives as an earthwork.

In the late 1960s the Great Pond was severed into two parts (now known as the North and South Ponds) by the construction of the section of the bypass between the Crown junction and the old Station roundabout (the junction of the B3035 and B2177 roads). The **South Pond**, which holds water all year round, was restored in the early 1970s and since then has been leased to the Bishop's Waltham Parish Fishing Club.

Bp. of Winchesters House, at Waltham, Hants.

Top: A 1784 engraving of the view across the Pond to the main range of Palace buildings that had been ruined in the Civil War 140 years earlier. (Copy of engraving courtesy of Jane Gentry).

Bottom: Quite remarkably, the view from the same spot in 2011, across what is now the South Pond, is instantly recognisable. (Copyright Colin Waterworth, Capcha Photography).

By contrast, the **North Pond** has suffered years of neglect. It is a seasonal Pond, with a permeable base, the water level rising and falling with the groundwater in the chalk aquifer, further influenced by the abstraction of water at the Northbrook Pumping Station half a mile to the north. Consequently the Pond holds water for some of the year but is dry for the remaining months, the timing dependent on the rainfall and abstraction patterns. Left unchecked, the Pond bed has been encroached upon by trees and scrub, as the natural tendency is to become wet woodland.

Because the North Pond is regarded by the community as an important natural asset, and the improvement to the Pond the top priority for environmental action, the North Pond Conservation Group was formed in 2010 to restore the Pond. In the first year, many trees were cleared from the Pond bed, through the efforts of volunteer work parties and with help from the Environment Agency. As a result there are extensive views across the Pond. In the next phases of the Restoration Plan, two viewing areas are to be created, and information panels provided.

The footbridge

In the early 1990s planning permission was given for the redevelopment of the Brewery Mill site in Lower Lane for a housing estate, subsequently known as St Bonnet Drive. Because the site had a substantial frontage to the North Pond, the planning agreement passed the ownership of the adjoining part of the Pond from private hands to Winchester City Council and provided the Council with sufficient funding to construct a footbridge across the Pond.

Top: The North Pond, viewed from the B2177 causeway in the spring of 2011, after the first phase of restoration.

Bottom left: A new footbridge was constructed across the Pond in the summer of 1992. Unfortunately it was built too low, and became flooded as soon as the Pond re-filled!

Bottom right: The footbridge was quickly rebuilt by the Council at a higher level and has served the town well, in particular providing people living on the west side of Bishop's Waltham with a more direct and attractive route in and out of the town centre. It is also a good place for people to pause and enjoy a remarkably rural setting close to the centre of the town.

Abbey Mill

Abbey Mill was built as a water-powered corn mill in 1862, on the dam that formed the Great Pond, the wheels being driven by water from that ancient fish pond. The ownership of the Mill changed hands several times before it was acquired by James Duke, whose company owned it for most of the 20th century.

After it ceased to be used as a mill it was used as offices, and the land behind it as an industrial estate. In 2003 planning permission was granted for housing on the site of the industrial estate and renewed permission was granted in 2008 for a revised plan that allowed for 70 houses (including 23 affordable homes) along with flexible business units and new office space. However, the developer did not proceed and the Mill and its surrounding land, as well as South Pond, were acquired by Sainsbury's in late 2008.

Their intention is to restore and convert the Mill building for use as staff offices, with three apartments, and use it as an entrance into the superstore proposed to be built on the land to the rear.

Top: Abbey Mill viewed from the east around 1900. Outside are workmen posing for the camera, and some horse-drawn wagons. The single storey building to the right of the Mill was Rooke's cycle and motor cycle works; above it can be seen the houses in Martin Street.

Centre: The Mill buildings in June 1970, the horse-drawn wagons having been replaced by a Duke's lorry. On the main building the larger of the two projecting gables still exists, but the smaller one has been removed. The former Rooke's workshop building has been given a second storey. Both buildings are, by this time, used as offices.

Bottom: The buildings from a similar viewpoint in the autumn of 2010, boarded up and awaiting the planning decision regarding the proposal for a Sainsbury's superstore on the site. The plans were approved in April 2011 by Winchester City Council.

Winchester Road

Winchester Road dates from the 1830s when the Bishop's Waltham to Fishers Pond turnpike road was constructed. Until then, the route going west from the town was a trackway serving farms.

Top: The OS 6" map of 1910 shows Winchester Road heading from the Station north west to the cross roads where roads go to Durley (south) and Ashton (north). The Claylands Brick & Tile Works is prominent at the end of Claylands Road, and workers' housing can be seen along Winchester and Victoria Roads. The more 'up-market' housing of the 1890s spreads along Avenue and Park Roads, and further west are larger houses such as Highfield, The Hermitage and The Hawthorns with access from Winchester Road. Everywhere else there are fields.

Bottom: The 2001 1/10000 map shows the great extent to which Bishop's Waltham has developed westwards in the 20th century, mainly since the 1960s, with housing estates spread along the north side of Winchester Road as far as the Ashton Lane junction, and along the south side as far as Albany Farm.

Facing page top left: Mr West's butcher's cart at the junction of Sawmill Lane (now Pondside Lane) and Winchester Road, c1917. Behind the horse are buildings associated with the sawmill. Pondside Lane is on the right. At the bottom of the hill the siding from the Station crossed the lane to the brickyard at Claylands.

Facing page bottom left: The sawmill disappeared long ago, and for at least the last two decades of the 20th century the site was occupied by a fish and chip shop and its car park. The site was redeveloped for housing around 2008.

Facing page top right: Elim Lodge (pictured in 2006) was the first house on the right on Winchester Road, heading west out of the town. It was a fine villa, probably built just after the First World War. The land behind Elim Lodge was J.E. Smith's coal yard, next to Bishop's Waltham Station, in the latter days of the railway. For at least the last 20 years of the 20th century the yard was a depot for Asphaltic, now based on Claylands Road.

Facing page bottom right: Regrettably, because Elim Lodge was not a listed building and situated outside the Conservation Area, it succumbed to pressures for redevelopment soon after the previous photograph was taken, together with the adjoining depot and yard. The new development of private apartments and affordable housing by Linden Homes is named Elim Close and is generally considered to be well designed for its prominent site by the main roundabout.

Avenue Road (later The Avenue) and Park Road were laid out in the 1890s as a better class residential area for successful tradesmen and professionals. Most houses were built between 1895 and 1910, and included semi-detached villas with generous sized gardens. The roads and footpaths remained unmade for many years.

Facing page top left: *Park Road, from Avenue Road, c1910. The two roads formed the major part of the late 19th century development in this area to the west of the earlier development at Newtown.*

Facing page bottom left: *For many years the view remained unchanged until the road was made up and more houses built on the right hand side.*

Facing page top right: *Park Road from the western end, as it was in 1963 soon after the road had been made up, even though the free range hen provides a rural note.*

Facing page bottom right: *In 2011 the view is similar, although the former field on the right is now occupied by houses (Mallard Close).*

Top: *This photograph was taken In March 1974 from the same spot as the image on the opposite page (Top right) but by turning around 180 degrees. The houses on the skyline are in Albany Road.*

Bottom: *From the same viewpoint in 2011, the fields are now occupied by houses, with Siskin Close roughly on the same alignment as the track in the earlier view. Siskin Close was built in 1986/7 as part of the Abbey Meadows development.*

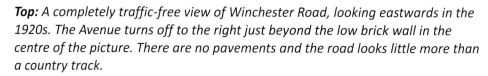

Top: *A completely traffic-free view of Winchester Road, looking eastwards in the 1920s. The Avenue turns off to the right just beyond the low brick wall in the centre of the picture. There are no pavements and the road looks little more than a country track.*

Bottom: *In 2011, this view is quite similar, except that the road was tarmacked long ago, and pavements provided. The house in the centre of the earlier picture, on the east side of the junction with The Avenue, is now Newtown Stores.*

Facing page top left: *Albany Road from near the junction with Winchester Road, probably in the early 1960s, when it was still an unmade road.*

Facing page bottom left: *In 2011 the road looks much smarter. The main change is that the field on the right, with the horse looking over the hedge, is now occupied by a small housing estate (Albany Court).*

Facing page top right: *Taken in the early 1960s looking westwards along Winchester Road from near the junction with Albany Road. On the right, the building being demolished is The Hermitage (formerly known as Pepperbox House).*

Facing page bottom right: *The Hermitage Heights housing estate was built on the site and surrounding land. The taller building beyond the terrace of houses is The Hawthorns, a block of flats that was built in the mid-1980s on the site of the house with the same name.*

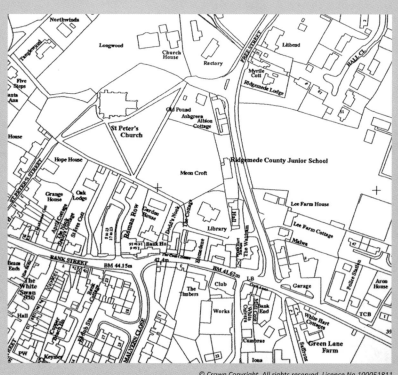

Bank Street East

Bank Street is named after Gunners Bank, but from medieval times had been known as French Street, possibly because French merchants traded here. There have been a few changes in the eastern part of Bank Street.

Top: The 25" map of the 1870s shows the area to the north-east of the town centre. Bank Street runs eastwards to a junction of roads, around which there are several old buildings. This cluster of buildings is believed to be the nucleus of a hamlet of some significance, possibly pre-dating the town. There were at least two medieval inns - the White Hart and the Wheatsheaf - which may indicate a significant amount of traffic. From this junction Free Street runs northwards, Hoe Road goes to the east, and Green Lane and Shore Lane towards the south. Free Street and Green Lane may have been part of the original line of the road between Winchester and Fareham.

Bottom: The 2001 version of the 1/2500 scale map shows that housing development has occurred to the south and south west of the hamlet, joining it to the town centre. The Library (formerly a school) and Church Hall are situated close to the junction, but there are no longer any pubs.

Facing page top left: The view westwards from near the brow of the hill in the 1920s. On the immediate left of the picture can be seen the projecting window to Locke's shop, a fish and game merchants shop until the 1960s. It was housed in a timber-framed medieval hall house dating from the 15th century or earlier. Beyond on the left is The White Swan public house, rebuilt in the early 1900s following demolition of a much older pub.

Facing page bottom left: The same view in 2011. The hall house is now a dwelling (Moysents) and the former White Swan pub is now flats and an Indian restaurant called Friends.

Facing page top right: Taken in April 1973, the house on the left behind the low brick wall is Church House, formerly Holm Oak, once the home of the Gunners (bankers and solicitors). Gunners Bank itself occupied part of the grey 19th century building immediately beyond. It had opened in 1809, and is now locally famous as the last private bank in England to produce its own bank notes; it closed in 1953.

Facing page bottom right: Church House and part of the house immediately to the east were demolished in the mid-1980s and replaced by Roman Row, sheltered housing accommodation.

BANK STREET, BISHOP'S WALTHAM.

On this page is a sequence of views looking westwards along Bank Street from the junction with Free Street and Hoe Road.

Top: *Mr Cutler, the blacksmith, standing outside his shop beside the White Hart Inn c1897; an inn had been on the site since the mid-1400s. Within a year the Institute would be built on the walled field opposite. Beyond that field is The Timbers, a 16th century oak framed building that still exists, as do the timber framed cottages on the roadside further on.*

Centre: *Taken from a similar viewpoint a few years later (c1912) after The Institute was built. On the left of the picture can be seen the shop window in the building on the eastern corner of the Bank Street/Shore Lane junction. Once it had been Etheridge's bakery shop and then Frank Wild's saddlery. The name of the pub changed from the White Hart to the Mafeking Hero in 1901, to mark the relief of the siege of Mafeking during the Boer War.*

Bottom: *The same view in 2011. The Mafeking Hero closed in 1989, since when it has been the Waltham Tandoori restaurant. The shop next to the Shore Lane junction is now a private residence. The railings along the Bank Street frontage of the Institute have been removed for road widening.*

Above: *The Institute was built in 1898 as an educational establishment (though never a school), providing a library and reading room, and technical classes for local people; its function as a centre for adult education ceased in 1961 when Swanmore Secondary School was built. It has served different purposes since; for example, as a Public Baths until the 1970s, then it housed a snooker club, and a baby clinic, as well as a local collection of antiquities that later became the basis of the Bishop's Waltham Museum in 1987. It closed completely in 2001.*

Top right: *The 2011 view shows that visually the Institute has not changed much, but it has been converted into flats.*

Right: *The archway and gallery at the White Hart Inn in the early 1900s. The building on the right was the Inn's stables.*

Far right: *The archway and a renewed gallery above still exist in 2011. The former stables are now used mainly as offices.*

Free Street

The origin of the name Free Street is not certain. Possibly it is so called because people could avoid the turnpike road charges by using this route through the town, but it is probable that the name Free Street pre-dates the introduction of turnpike roads.

Facing page top left: The junction of Bank Street and Free Street in March 1962. On the left is the Mafeking Hero public house. On the far side of the junction is the picturesque group of 17th century cottages that once housed the Wheatsheaf public house (which probably closed before 1910).

Facing page bottom left: In 2011 the view is very similar, although the Mafeking Hero sign has been replaced by the Waltham Tandoori's, literally a sign of the times! The petrol pumps have gone from the Village Garage, and on the field beyond a dentists' surgery and the Police Station have been built.

Facing page top right: A lovely sepia-tinted view of Free Street from the junction with Bank Street and Hoe Road. On the far left is the Mafeking Hero. Beyond, alongside the road, is the old Mission Hall, which became redundant when St Paul's Church was built in 1910. On the right are Wheatsheaf cottages; the entrance to the bar in the former Wheatsheaf public house was through the door on the extreme right of the photograph.

Facing page bottom right: The same view in 2011, the Mission Hall and adjoining cottage having been demolished in 1966 for road widening. Free Street might be wider and safer now, but its country lane feel has been lost and its use as a 'rat run' all too common.

Top: Free Street, looking towards Bank Street, about 1905. A dog stands in the gateway to Lee's farmyard. Further along the road, cattle are passing the Wheatsheaf Inn. In the centre is the cottage adjoining the Mission Hall beyond. The track in the right foreground goes past the Church Hall to the Mafeking Hero, the archway and open gallery of which can be seen in the distance.

Bottom: In the 2011 view the main change is that the Mission Hall and cottage have been demolished, and the site now forms a not very functional open space between the Church Hall and the widened road. It is highly unlikely that cattle would be seen walking along Free Street these days!

Facing page top left: *The Free Street School in the 1920s. It was built in 1896 as a school for infants, replacing the old National School which stood in St Peter's churchyard (see map on page 12). However, when Newtown School opened the infants were moved there and this became the boys' school. In later years it catered for 7 to 15 year-old children until Swanmore Secondary School opened in 1962.*

Facing page bottom left: *Although the building became redundant, it lives on as the town's Library and local Registration Office, as well as accommodating the Little Petals Children's Centre. Some of the playground walls and the school gates have now gone.*

Facing page top right: *The Church Hall from the approach road in 1913.*

Facing page bottom right: *Surprisingly, a century later, the view is very similar, although the Church Hall has been extended and the forbidding high entrance wall replaced with a more welcoming low wall. The Library (Bottom left) is in the background. The yew trees show almost 100 years of growth.*

Top: *Maypole Green in 1913, so called because until the 17th century there was a maypole here. When the Maypole Cottages were demolished, the materials were reused to build a house called Old Pound on the same site (named after the pound for stray animals that used to be on the green).*

Bottom: *After damaging subsidence, the Old Pound has, in turn, been replaced by another house, completed in 2011. The once grassy triangle, where the maypole stood is now a tarmac parking area, and a pavement has been added.*

80

Northbrook

Northbrook House has a fascinating history.

It was built in the late 1700s as a fine Georgian mansion, and was used as a private home by a succession of owners until sold to Droxford Rural District Council for use as the Council's headquarters, until the Council ceased to exist following local government reorganisation in 1974. In 1976 it was acquired by Husband & Co., a firm of civil engineers and architects, who were involved in a wide range of construction projects around the world. After they left, Northbrook House remained vacant for many years. Then Linden Homes and Breamore Developments acquired it in 2001 and set about sensitively converting into luxury flats the House and the west wing (which had been constructed by Husband & Co. in the mid-1970s); they also built dwellings in the grounds.

Facing page left: A plan of the Northbrook estate when it was sold by auction in 1922 by Richard Austin & Wyatt (who remain an estate agency in Bishop's Waltham, in The Square). At that time, the estate included three plots with cottages on the west side of Lower Lane. When the estate had been sold eleven years earlier, the sales particulars referred to Northbrook House as being in a "good residential district near the meets of several packs of hounds". Also, the estate included other plots of land in the area.

Facing page right: The modern 1/2500 scale map (2001) shows that Bishop's Waltham House nursing home has been built in the grounds of the estate. The junction of Free Street and Lower Lane has been staggered to provide a safer crossroads with Beeches Hill. Across the road, a house has been built in Butt's Dell, light industrial buildings occupy the chalk pit and Colville Drive and Hall Close have been built on what was Butt's Farm.

Top: The owners of Northbrook House, Mr and Mrs Bamforth, standing in the entrance porch with nurses during the First World War, when the Bamforths allowed the House to be used as an infirmary for wounded soldiers.

Bottom: The rear of Northbrook House, c1918.

Top: *The impressive Georgian front of Northbrook House as it was in 1950, when it was used by Droxford Rural District Council.*

Bottom: *The modern view shows that little has changed, other than the vegetation, and the recent conversion to multiple residential use has been carried out with care.*

Facing page top left: *The northern end of Free Street, c1910, leading down to Lower Lane. On the left in the distance is Northbrook Farm, with its granary on staddle stones, accessed from Beeches Hill.*

Facing page bottom left: *The modern view from roughly the same viewpoint. As mentioned on page 81, the junction with Lower Lane and Beeches Hill is now very busy and has been realigned for safety reasons. Northbrook Farm (now growing vines) is hidden behind the trees around the 40 mph sign.*

Facing page top right: *The 'water splash' at Northbrook, c1910. This area of water, where the North Brook flows under the road at the bottom of Beeches Hill, was popular with children for paddling and catching small fish, as well as being used by horses for drinking. In the centre is the junction with the Corhampton to Bishop's Waltham road, and in the top right of the picture Northbrook House can be seen through the trees. Beyond the watersplash is Northbrook Villa.*

Facing page bottom right: *The water splash dried up long ago, perhaps because of the abstraction of water at Northbrook Pumping Station that was needed to meet the demands of the increasing population in the area. The pool of water and the nearby watercress beds have gone, to be replaced by a patch of wetland vegetation and tall scrub.*

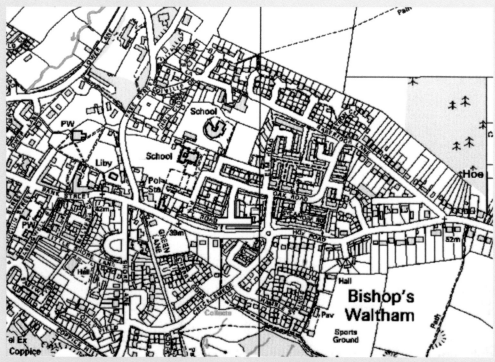

Hoe Road and Ridgemede

Going east towards Swanmore from the Bank Street/Free Street junction is Hoe Road, so called because it served Lower Hoe, West Hoe and Little Hoe Farms. The area north of Hoe Road has become known as Ridgemede after the house of the same name. Until the early 1960s Hoe Road and Ridgemede were very rural but in the past 50 years there has been extensive development.

Top: *The 6" map of 1910 shows the road to Swanmore (now known as Hoe Road) heading east from Bishop's Waltham and Rareridge Lane connecting it with Free Street, opposite Northbrook House. Adjoining Rareridge Lane (though with its main access from Free Street) is Ridgemede, a fine house built by C. R. Gunner in 1897 for his family. For many years most of the land within the triangle bounded by Free Street, Rareridge Lane and the Swanmore road belonged to Ridgemede.*

Bottom: *The 2001 version of the 1/10000 scale map shows that the whole of the triangle has been built on, in order to provide the current Junior and Infants Schools, the extensive Ridgemede Council Estate and the private housing estates of Colville Drive and Hall Close. Land on the north side of Rareridge Lane has also been developed for housing.*

Facing page top left: *Ridgemede House, c1903, with Mr Lewis cutting hay, using the horse-drawn mower within the grounds.*

Facing page bottom left: *Because private housing has been built in the grounds to the south-west of Ridgemede House, a comparable view is impossible. Ridgemede House is now sheltered accommodation for the elderly.*

Facing page top right: *The view along the Swanmore Road from the Free Street/Bank Street junction, c1905. The barn on the left used to be part of Lees Farm. The sign belongs to the Wheatsheaf Inn (see page 76), just out of the picture to the left. On the extreme right is the entrance to Green Lane, then White Hart Cottage (early 18th century), and beyond is the building used by the blacksmith Mr Cutler after he moved from the White Hart (see page 74).*

Facing page top left: *Much has changed apart from the continuing presence of White Hart Cottage. The barn and farmyard have long gone, and the Village Garage, Whites dentists, and a Police Station stand in their place. Beyond is the extensive Ridgemede housing estate, built in the 1960s.*

Top: *Mr and Mrs Ernest Lewis stand outside their house on the Ridgemede estate on their Golden Wedding anniversary in April 1968. Mr Lewis remembered that one of his first jobs was minding sheep on this land, for 6d a day! It is quite possible that this is the same Mr Lewis who was mowing hay on page 85. The relatively new houses in Willow Road are prominent.*

Bottom: *Many years later, the houses in Willow Road are still in good condition and well looked after, and the estate's appearance has been enhanced by the growth of trees.*

Facing page top left: *Houses in Pine Road in April 1965, soon after the new occupants had settled in. The houses were built to a good standard with gardens of a reasonable size, and the estate was provided with a network of tarmac roads and pavements.*

Facing page bottom left: *By 2011 many houses had new porches and windows, and the care given to front gardens is evident.*

Facing page top right: *Ridgemede Junior School under construction in 1969, with houses in Oak Road visible to the right. It was built by Faulkners of Waterlooville for around £90,000. Officially opened in May 1970, it was designed to provide for 320 children.*

Facing page bottom right: *More than 40 years later the main School building is within a setting of mature trees, and in the foreground a small amphitheatre has been constructed for the children to perform plays. The school is now known as Bishop's Waltham Junior School.*

The Moors

The Moors was designated as a Site of Special Scientific Interest (SSSI) in 1979 because of its range of wetland habitats and species, making it one of the best inland wetland sites in Hampshire.

Of its particular type of habitat, calcareous fen meadow, it is one of the most botanically rich in the UK. The breadth of species is due to the site's location at the junction of the clay beds and the chalk, and hence the unusual combination of chalk (alkaline) water emerging from the springs on to a site where the soil is basically acidic. As a result the site is home to chalk species like milkwort and cowslips, as well as acidic species such as heathers, orchids and tormentil.

About 17 hectares (40 acres) of the western and central parts of the SSSI were acquired by Hampshire County Council (HCC), with support from the Bishop's Waltham Society, in 1988. Since then the area has been managed by HCC's Countryside Service as a Local Nature Reserve in order to improve its value for nature conservation. As part of its management of the site the Council has, with the help of volunteer work parties, reversed the encroachment of woodland on to the eastern fen. Because the operation of the Hoe Pumping Station was found to be having a damaging drawdown effect on the water levels and wetland flora and fauna in the SSSI, the Pumping Station was closed in 2003.

Top: The 6" scale map of 1910 shows The Moors in open countryside, as a mostly open area with several springs and water channels converging on the Mill Pond. There are also a couple of watercress beds within The Moors. On the other side of the road from the Mill Pond is Chase (or Waltham) Mill. The stream that flows south west from the Mill joins the stream from Northbrook just south of Bishop's Waltham, to form the River Hamble.

Bottom: On the 1/10000 scale map of 2000 it can be seen that the built-up area of Bishop's Waltham has extended to the western and northern edges of The Moors, which has become more wooded through lack of grazing. The watercress beds have disappeared, possibly due to the increasing abstraction of water for the public water supply and other uses, causing the springs to dry up or become unreliable.

Above: The chalk water offered ideal conditions for growing watercress. The photograph shows Peppler's watercress beds on The Moors near Suetts Farm, c1920, with George Peppler and an assistant pausing from their work to look at the camera. The site is now too overgrown to photograph.

Top right: Where the spring emerges on the western edge of the site, near Godfrey Pink Way, there is a feature called the Sandboils, caused by spring water bubbling up through the sandy bed of a shallow pond.

Bottom right: As part of the 'Water for Life' week in June 1998, HCC's Countryside Service organised an open day at The Moors that was visited by nearly 1000 people. Local (now national) celebrity Chris Packham opened the event and is seen here encouraging children to explore the delights of pond dipping.

Mill Pond and Chase Mill

Within The Moors Local Nature Reserve is the former mill pond that was managed to provide water to turn the wheels of Chase Mill, on the other side of the Bishop's Waltham to Wickham road.

Because of lack of management for perhaps three decades, the pond had become silted up. After acquiring the site, Hampshire County Council's Countryside Service dredged the mill pond to improve its value for nature conservation and to enable the Mill to be operated again.

Top: *The Mill Pond in the early 1900s with the Wickham Road on the left.*

Bottom: *More than a century later, little has changed. The information panel has been installed by the County Council's Countryside Service to explain the importance of the site and the way it is managed for wildlife.*

The mill on the road to Wickham, opposite The Moors, has been known variously as Waltham Mill, Chase Mill and Waltham Chase Mill over the years. To complicate matters further, it possibly stands on the site of East Mill, recorded in the 14th century. The present one is a Victorian twin pitchback mill. It was used to mill grain for animal feed and to produce flour for baking.

It was operated by two overshot water-wheels fed by a metal trough or leat from the Mill Pond on The Moors. The mill was last operated commercially in 1957, but in the 1990s its new owner, Dr Jeremy Nedwell, carried out partial restoration and has occasionally held open days at which the mill has been operated, and produced flour again.

Above: The cluster of mill buildings next to the road to Wickham, with the Georgian Mill House, a Grade 2* listed building, beyond. The main mill building is the one at right angles to the road.

Top right: The main mill building in 2010, the two water wheels (the one on the left has been restored), and the metal trough that carries water to the wheels from the Mill Pond.

Bottom right: The old sign that used to be above the main entrance.

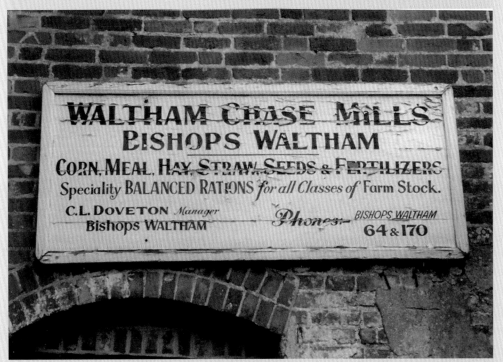

Gallery

Top: *The High Street on 30ᵗʰ December 1895, when the Friendship Lodge of the Oddfellows opened their new hall (in the background to the left of the banner). The town band and most of the population turned out for the occasion. The Oddfellows Hall is now The King's Church.*

Bottom: *HM The Queen and HRH Prince Philip pass through Bishop's Waltham on a wet day in 1959, on their way from Winchester to Portsmouth.*

Facing page top: *A works outing from the Claylands Brick and Tile Works, probably c1890. The assembled company marched off to the Railway Station accompanied by the town band. The special train, decorated for the occasion, took them to Bournemouth. In the background of the picture are buildings in the new settlement of Newtown. On the skyline to the right of the banner are houses in Victoria and Albert Roads, Newtown School (with the small spire), and The Priory. On the right in the middle distance is the Railway Inn (now the Priory Inn).*

Facing page bottom: *The people of Bishop's Waltham celebrated the Queen's Silver Jubilee in June 1977 in a variety of activities. This cheerful group is assembled outside the Barleycorn Inn, Basingwell Street.*

Page 94: *Charlie Tilbury, standing in Shore Lane with J. H. Morris's milk float in the early 1900s. The milk has come from Butts Farm, off Free Street. Beyond the horse is Iona Cottage. On the left, in the distance, are the Institute and the archway of the Mafeking Hero public house in Bank Street.*

Page 95: *Station Road, looking towards St George's Square, c1908. On the left are the livery stables that were situated in the Palace Mews. The liveried coach man in the pony and trap (centre) appears to be waiting for the photographer and his smart lady friend, who is holding another camera, to finish taking the picture. It is to early photographers like this that this book owes so much. On the right is part of the wall around the Palace ruins. The first building on the right was the old Fire Engine house.*

Back cover: *A "panoricard" (panoramic postcard) of Bank Street (on the left) and Free Street, c1912. In the centre is the Mafeking Hero public house and opposite, on the left, is the Institute.*

The Bishop's Waltham Society

The Bishop's Waltham Society (BWS) was formed as a Civic Society in 1986 with the following purposes:

1) To promote high standards of both planning and architecture.

2) To inform the public about the geography, history, natural history and architecture in the area.

3) To secure the preservation, protection, development and improvement of features of historic or public interest.

One of the main functions of the BWS has been that of 'environmental watchdog'. It has closely monitored planning applications and made representations to Winchester City Council, and other planning authorities, on proposals that would affect the character of the town. One of its early successes was to save Southbrook House, in Brook Street, from demolition. An outwardly Victorian house, it concealed a much older building that was subsequently conserved.

The Society has also been vigilant when there has been public consultation on local plans for the area.

Over the years the BWS has organised numerous talks and guided walks on subjects of interest, and has occasionally staged exhibitions. In the early days the Society had an active group of conservation volunteers, who planted native trees and shrubs alongside the B3035 Corhampton Road, and bulbs on roadside verges. These initiatives spawned such successful ventures as the Best Kept Village and Bishop's Waltham in Bloom schemes.

The group also installed barn owl boxes around the parish to help to reverse the decline of this popular species. One of the most successful projects undertaken by the BWS was to secure the opening up of a public footpath along the disused railway line (see page 55).

For membership information about the Bishop's Waltham Society please contact Tony Kippenberger by email at **bishopswalthamsociety@gmail.com** or by post at Gable House, Bank Street, Bishop's Waltham, Hampshire, SO32 1AE.

Above: Representatives of the Society receiving First Prize in Hampshire's Village Ventures Competition 1985-87, awarded in recognition of the breadth and depth of the Society's achievements in its first two years.

The awards were presented by Maldwin and Gilly Drummond (centre of picture), and the Society's representatives were the first three Chairmen: Trevor Harvey (second from right), Judith Fairhurst (third from left) and Alan Inder (extreme right).

The presentation took place in the Institute, in Bank Street, in 1988.